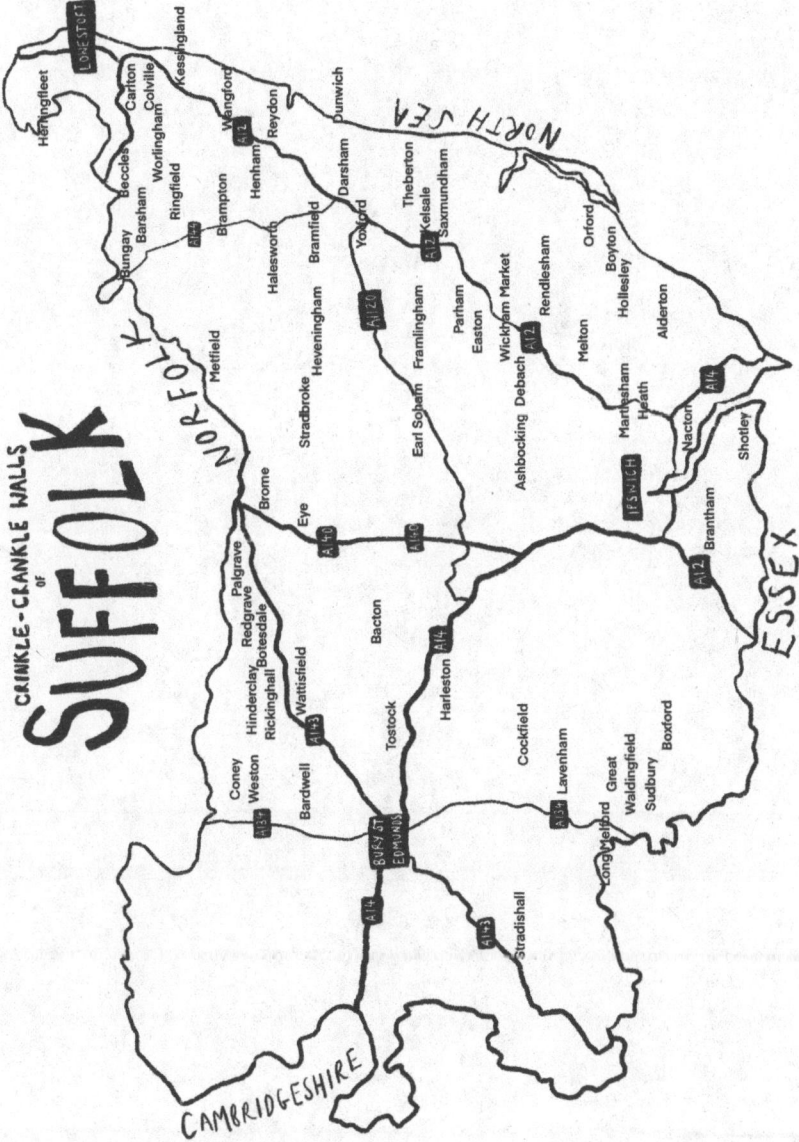

CRINKLE-CRANKLE WALLS
OF
SUFFOLK

The Crinkle-Crankle Crew

by Ed Broom

Published and Manufactured by Softwood Books
EU Responsible person: Maddy Glenn
Office 2, Wharfside House, Prentice Road, Stowmarket, Suffolk, IP14 1RD
www.softwoodbooks.com
hello@softwoodbooks.com

EU Rep:
Authorised Rep Compliance Ltd., Ground Floor, 71 Lower Baggot Street, Dublin, D02 P593,
Ireland
www.arccompliance.com
info@arccompliance.com

Paperback ISBN: 978-1-0369-2960-2

Notes

There are some fabulous crinkle-crankle walls easily visible from the road or public footpath such as those at Easton, Bramfield and Eye. Others, which I've marked as private, are hidden away. Please respect the privacy of those property owners.

Cover design and map illustration by Rose Broom.

For photos, please search for "thecrinklecranklecrew" on Instagram.

~ 2015 ~

Chapter 1

Late August in 2015, a fine summer's evening, and my back was to the wall.

For weeks I'd been trying and failing to come up with an idea for a short story. Anything half-decent would be fine. At this stage of the game, though, some smaller fraction would be more than acceptable. Like a distant steam train, the deadline that had once appeared so far away, no more than a tiny puff of smoke, was now fast approaching the station. I wasn't on the platform. I didn't have a ticket. I was still outside searching for a place to lock my bike.

Entries for the competition (run by the glossy *Suffolk* magazine) were due in by the end of the month. Two and a bit days to go and not a single word written of the 1500 expected.

"Each entry," said the blurb on page 59, "must have a strong connection with Suffolk."

Fair enough. Always preferable to have a topic on which to focus the mind. What do we have in this here county?

The coast? Beach huts? Second homes? Southwold?

Fields? Flatness? Flat fields. A Suffolk punch in a flat field?

Churches? Being in the east? Eastern churches?

And so on and so forth, every tired idea the subject of a thousand picture postcards. What I wanted was something different, something original, something curious. With that last word in mind, my Googling steered me towards a Wikipedia page, part of which said:

"The county of Suffolk claims at least 50 examples, twice as many as in the whole of the rest of the country."

Ooh. Promising. Most promising. Which brought me to late August 2015 with my back against the wall. A different, original, curious kind of wall. A crinkle-crankle wall.

1

It wasn't just me admiring the masonry. Determined to see one in the flesh, as it were, I thought others might be interested.

"Hey, kids," I'd said at tea-time, sounding like a complete dad, "who wants to come out and see an actual crinkle-crankle wall? Nana's coming, by the way."

Their eyes told me what I needed to know. A hard pass from Eldest daughter, about to head round a friend's, and another from The Boy, Xbox FIFA crazy.

"I hear the sofa calling," said my supportive wife.

"I'll come," said a reluctant daughter. Praise be for middle children. Picking up my mum ten minutes later, we left Ipswich, took the A12 past Woodbridge then turned off near Wickham Market. Some bendy roads carried us to the village of **Easton (#1)**. Please drive slowly, said the sign.

With the White Horse pub in my rear-view mirror, an astonishing sight appeared to our right. Convention dictates that a brick wall be flat. Straight. Dull. Like a sheet of uncooked lasagne. Not this one. Honestly, it became a little hard to concentrate on the road as the wall weaved its wobbly way alongside us. In, out, in, out, its curves continuing around the corner.

Should you Google this particular structure, you'll likely chance across a BBC news story from May 2014 headed *"Easton crinkle-crankle wall restored after crash."* One Friday evening in November 2013, an unknown motorist crashed into the wall. Did they stop? No, they did not, leaving the poor owner to have some difficult discussions with his insurance company. Total cost of repairs using properly vintage materials was the best part of twenty thousand pounds.

Anyway, we parked nearby and crossed to view the beast close up. As we stood on the grass verge, it towered over all of us. Rows and more rows and yet more rows of individual bricks, shorts and longs, assembled in a way to play with your mind. I ran my fingers along the well-weathered roughness. It felt old and somehow wise, like your grandmother's face when you're a child. And when there were no passing cars and nobody was watching, I folded my arms and rolled along it, a bottle bobbing on a gentle wave.

My mum took some photos. My mum always takes photos. Then our little trio followed the wall's path back towards the pub. Just short of All Saints Church, there's a break with a fancy gateway. People live behind the wall, note. Then it picks up again before, appropriately enough, finishing in the graveyard. David Coleman's ghostly voice whispered in my ear that this was truly quite remarkable.

From the early 1700s, Easton was home to the Earl of Rochford. After his father died in 1781, one William Henry Nassau de Zuylestein became the fifth and final owner of that title. It was Bill, as his friends no doubt called him, who decided to commission a fashionable serpentine wall around his sizeable estate: two miles long, over eight feet tall.

"This," I announced to the generations above and below, "is meant to be the longest crinkle-crankle wall. In the world!" Pause. "Or so says the internet." Middler, my daughter, could represent Suffolk at the National Indifference Championships if she could be bothered to enter. My mum, who'd passed this way several times over the years, was impressed.

I had a minor obsession at that time with The Swimmer, a 1964 short story written by John Cheever and published by *The New Yorker*. Neddy, the central character, sunbathing at a friend's, realises that he can get home by cutting through a series of back gardens and that he'll take a dip in every pool. Perhaps I could adapt the plot and have somebody head back past a series of crinkle-crankle walls, rolling along each one in turn? The mighty Burt Lancaster starred in the film version. In the BBC adaptation of my unwritten tale, I envisioned someone like David Morrissey or Jason Isaacs (hello!) in the lead role. That was Easton, home of the mother wall, the sovereign of serpentines, what we might call the ur-crinkle-crankle. The webpage, I recalled, had mentioned 50 or so others. I've always lived in Suffolk, ditto my mum, and neither of us could name another example. Where on earth were the rest?

Chapter 2

Despite Wikipedia's blather about "the many crinkle-crankle walls found in East Anglia" and Suffolk's half-century, the only one actually named within the article was Easton: been there, done that. Spend as much time on Wikipedia as me and you'll be familiar with the phrase "citation needed". You say there are at least 50: where's your proof?

However, that web page did include a terrific photo of one other local example in somewhere called **Bramfield (#2)**. I say "terrific" because the viewpoint is a few feet above the coping – the top course of the wall – and shows it slithering away into the middle distance. Also apparent is the scrawniness of the structure: one brick thick. Credit to the snapper, Nat Bocking, who I knew online from his love of seaplanes, his work with local film productions and his contributions to the British Water Tower Appreciation Society.

Bramfield, I didn't know. Bramford, I did. An ever-expanding village barely outside of Ipswich, I'd often bike down there of a Saturday morning to see my future best man. Five minutes' pedalling along the rutted track starting from the end of Bramford Lane in IP1 would bring you out by the haunted house at the head of the village. Well, that was the case until the A14 cruelly bisected that route.

So, not Bramford but Bramfield. Still grappling for a short story idea – the metaphorical train had pulled into platform 2 and doors would close thirty seconds before departure – I raised the prospect of a second outing with the family. Generous chap that I am, we'd had Sunday lunch at Jimmy's Farm. Where better to walk it off than Bramfield?

"Drop me at home first," said my wife.

"Ditto," said my son.

Nice to know where you stand. Which left me, the girls and my mum.

Once more unto the A12, dear friends, once more; or close the wall up! At Darsham, the Lowestoft railway line crosses the road. One minute later, there's a hard-to-miss black and white arrow pointing left towards Halesworth and Bungay on the A144. Bramfield features in the small print.

Thanks to my ex-membership of the 24th Ipswich Scout Group, I was prepared, aware that the wall was opposite the church, and vice versa. Seeing the 30mph sign, we scanned both sides of The Street assuming that the church would reveal itself. Exiting the village, it hadn't.

One U-turn later, we undertook a second pass. I guessed and took a left into Bridge Street. Hello, school. Hello, village hall. No obvious place of worship. Another three point turn and, pausing at The Street, we went straight over past The Queen's Head into Walpole Road. Woah, behold.

To our right in the late afternoon haze, the impressive Grade I listed church of St Andrew complete with odd outbuilding, "the only detached round tower in Suffolk" according to the encyclopaedic Simon Knott. To our left, the wibbliest-wobbliest wall you've ever seen. Weaving to and fro like a wino off the wagon, it threatens to topple down before your very eyes. At various times in its 200 year history, that's happened, judging by the odd mismatched patch of stretcher bond.

"Easton was good but I prefer this one," said my mum.

Bramfield has more than enough architectural antiquity to merit a Conservation Area Appraisal, section 12.4 of which describes "the long, tightly curved late 18th century serpentine walls." Tightly curved? Nice. Meanwhile, at the section nearest the pub, the wall blossoms and executes a sinuous 270 degree turn before continuing out of sight. No set squares here, ta very much.

Interrupting the wall is a flinted ornate gateway with steps up to an enticing door leading who knows where. Probably into the grounds of Bramfield Hall, keepers of the wall. Currently owned by Simon Robey – city trader and former chair of the Royal Opera House – the big house has its origins in the 1400s with the Rabett family. In common with the round tower, they're of Norman extraction. Those Rabetts had a good run, ending with the demise of Reverend Reginald Rabett who, belying the name, died without issue in 1860. His father, also Reginald, was the church warden at St Andrews over the road. Around 1790 Reginald Senior had the hall extended: odds-on that he also authorized the wall.

Pop into the church and you'll see a quartet of diamond-shaped hatchments, these being large tablets displaying the coat of arms of the recently deceased. These ones commemorate the Rabetts. Their heraldry, naturally, includes a set of bunny ears. Try as I might, I could not locate a male ancestor named Roger.

Our visit wouldn't have been complete without a vaguely irresponsible action on my part. I badly felt the need to shin up a tree on the grassy bank by the wall and, despite my mum's tutting, duly did so – nicely quiet on a Sunday – all the better to mimic Nat Bocking's Wikipedia image. Reginald's wall came out very well.

Driving home, the competition deadline 24 hours away, I revised the casting for my as-yet-to-be-written piece. Returning to that Cheever story, out went the British lead to be replaced by Ross from Friends, thus guaranteeing the funding. I imagined him making a film in deepest East Anglia and becoming lost, his only reference point being a weirdly shaped wall. Sitting at the dining table that evening, I prepared to pen my prize-winning fiction.

Chapter 3

Late one Friday evening in May of the previous year, the tranquillity disturbed only by the sighing of the dishwasher, I'd parked my bookish backside in that same chair. Aided by some notes scrawled on a 5x3 index card, I bashed out the tale of Manny, a boy obsessed with The Global Peace Index. Squeezing out the final scene about 3am, it took another hour to type up the half-dozen handwritten A4 sheets.

Saturday lunchtime – "Dad, you're up" – I printed it out and spent a satisfying couple of hours chopping this, changing that. I extracted The Boy mid-afternoon from a pixelated Anfield – "Do I have to?" – for a father-and-son drive to the coast. We parked, walked into the library and, at 4:45pm, I handed in my entry to the Felixstowe Book Festival short story competition for 2014. Gotta be in it to win it, ha!

Reader, I won it.

The point being, apart from seizing any chance to blow my own bugle, that I needed that pressure to write. I thrived on that pressure. With my inter-city standing at platform 4, the far side of the pedestrian bridge, I'm happiest discussing ticket options with the nice man at the desk. This time, though, I had a theme, a strong Suffolk theme – crinkle-crankle walls – but little else. You can't accuse someone of losing the plot if they've never had one. Don't dive into that pool, Ross; it's been drained. Take Marcel and fly back to Rachel.

"The competition closes on August 31 2015," said the opening sentence of the magazine's terms & conditions. That was one more than I'd managed. As it happened, that was a Bank Holiday. The day came and went, and at some point I accepted that it wasn't going to happen. Like that inflatable boy who toys with a safety pin, I'd let myself down.

Biking to work the next day, moving on, I resolved to bounce back. Pinch-punch and all that.

Step the first, I climbed back on the writing saddle by knocking together a tiny tale for a great little website called Paragraph Planet. *Suffolk* magazine wanted 1500 words. PP wanted 75 words exactly, title included. I could do that, and duly submitted my six sentence story about, um, a man biking to work. Write what you know. Two self-esteem points to me.

Step the second, idling on the internet, I found several sightings of a serpentine at Eye. One of those mentions was in the Suffolk volume of *The Buildings of England*, "the unrivalled series of comprehensive architectural guides" (their blurb) written by Nikolaus Pevsner. Looking up from my computer at home, there sat the actual black-edged book on my actual shelf. Handy.

Prolific Pevsner produced his premier Penguin pocket publication – Cornwall, if you're curious – in 1951, followed by Middlesex and Nottinghamshire in that same year. Armed with bundles of research notes, he toured Suffolk for only four weeks in August 1957, a month after Macmillan's "never had it so good" speech. As per his previous nationwide trips, his wife Lola did the driving (as he notes in the foreword) "with skill and patience". Work on umpteen other areas plus endless proof-reading and fact checking meant that the first edition of *Suffolk* wasn't published until 1961. One year later came the publication of *Norfolk*, not that it's a competition.

~~~~~~~

Imagining the Pevsners pootling around nearly 60 years ago put me in the mood for an impromptu Thursday evening outing. To my slight surprise, all previous participants signed up. Scooping up my mum – "This is becoming a habit!" – the Nissan Qashqai's robot brain switched on the lights. If the sequence 50-30-50-40-30 rings a bell, that may be because you've driven north on the A140 with its fickle speed limits. At The Auberge restaurant we swung right into Eye on the B1117, a prime route.

Learning from Bramfield, we went directly to the main drag near Lee's Cottage. Sounds quaint? That's the local Chinese takeaway.

"This way," I said, shepherding my flock (and their nana) along Lambseth Street. "Just up here, promise."

Opposite the alms-houses and past the fire station begins a lovely lengthy wall that I'd examined earlier that day on Google Street View. I moused my virtual car past the many alternating convex and concave sections, halted briefly at the gate to read the small plaque – **Chandos Lodge (#3)** – then carried on past the remaining curves before heading left at the corner into Castleton Way.

You may know that the priceless tool that is Street View sometimes displays a tiny clockface in the top left under the address. If so, you can travel in time and see earlier versions of that same scene. Playing with this, I spotted two blokes repairing part of the wall in January 2009, and more fellas working on a different stretch in July 2011. Storm damage? Careless motorists, like Easton?

Clive Paine's *History of Eye* tells us that "the house was designed in 1811 by Dent Hooper of Chelmsford" – I wasn't at school with anybody named Clive, let alone Dent – and that it's named after Elizabeth, Duchess of Chandos. Mr Paine doesn't remark further on the wall itself.

Dark by now, the photographers among us – me, my mum – waited for passing cars to provide illumination. According to my phone, I snapped my snap at 20:20, impeccable timing for low light conditions in downtown Eye.

Returning to the motor, I announced to my passengers' delighted faces that we weren't quite done yet. "Pevsner says there's another wall five minutes away." Five minutes later we pulled into the partially potholed driveway of a Best Western hotel named **Brome Grange (#4)**. Unclear where to look, Eldest and I (no other takers) sidled into the reception.

"Can I help you?" asked a smiling woman.

"Um, this might sound strange but we're looking for a crinkle-crankle wall...?"

Did she look askance? Did she call security? Neither of those things. "You want to see it? It's round the back. Follow me."

Through the foyer, down a corridor and out through a side door, she poked a finger into the darkness.

"Over there." She inclined her head. "Couples sometimes like to have their wedding photos taken against it if the sun's out. I'll leave you to it." And she was gone.

My eyes aren't the greatest – I wear specs to drive – and I'm not sure Eldest could make out a lot either. We wound our way back to the car, bumped around to the rear and directed our headlights towards where the nice lady had directed us. Not the greatest view, truth be told, yet whatever was out there was good enough to warrant a mention by the mighty Pevsner. Also, being out in the garden, it's beyond the remit of those Street View lenses.

~~~~~~~

Home that night, I grabbed my Pevsner *Suffolk* hardback and handed it to Eldest with a cup of tea.

"Since you've got some time on your hands…"

I got the inevitable look. She was about to return to university.

"…could you take a look at this, do some Googling and knock up a quick list of crinkle-crankles?"

Chapter 4

There's something very Practical Parenting about inventing a task for your child to complete. My search engine skills were decent but I was (and remain) way older than Eldest; she'd grown up with the internet and I hoped she might succeed where I'd failed.

See, in my real-life *Suffolk* book – the 1974 second edition – I'd unearthed an intriguing passage within the fifty page introduction. Pevsner talks of "the delightful CRINKLE-CRANKLE WALLS of Suffolk..." – his capitals – "...which Mr Norman Scarfe has collected and published."

A-ha! Like the Rabetts of Bramfield, that list was evidently of Norman origin. He then cites five locations, including Easton (been there) and Bramfield (done that), and adds a throwaway remark about "many other places*". The gall of that asterisk! Anyway, it leads to this footnote:

"*By the end of 1965 Mr Scarfe's count had reached fifty-six."

Makes sense, I thought. That would mostly align with Wikipedia's 50 examples. Bash that into Google, bish-bosh, and I'd be scrolling down that list before you could boil an egg. Not so fast, Delia.

One of the most promising search results led to an obituary in *The Independent* newspaper for a chap called George Coulson who'd died in January 1993. Skilled with languages, he worked on Enigma at Bletchley Park and later, living near Eye (!), he became involved with the Suffolk Preservation Society and "took on the listing and measurement of serpentine or crinkle-crankle walls of which the major proportion stand in Suffolk."

I found evidence of this in The Garden History Society Newsletter. Dated September 1971, an entry in the notes & queries section is headed "Serpentine, wavy or ribbon walls" and reads:

"Mr G.A. Coulson, of Yaxley Hall, Eye, Suffolk, is collecting information about the location of existing serpentine walls in this country. He would also like to know whether anyone knows anything about their origin and their date of introduction."

Good stuff. I was getting warmer. Then I noticed that the obituary had been compiled by none other than Norman Scarfe. All B-roads were winding their way towards one man. If you want to know about walls, ask Mr Scarfe.

I was no more than vaguely aware of Norman Scarfe. Having looked him up, I was a tad ashamed of that. Born in Felixstowe. Educated in Oxford. Involved in the D-day landings. Founded the Suffolk Records Society. First chair of the Suffolk Book League. Helped establish the Museum of East Anglian Life at Stowmarket. Chairman of the Centre of East Anglian Studies at UEA. A good egg.

He'd also written enough books to line the "local interest" shelf at Waterstones and at least four of those namechecked Suffolk in the title. Perhaps one included the "published" list of walls? Maybe, maybe not: I sure couldn't find it online, hence the request to Eldest.

Home after work on the Friday, seven days after our Easton excursion, I was midway through the sentence "How did you get on with that…" when Eldest slid a piece of paper across the dining table.

"Walls," she added, a trifle redundantly. Torn from a reporter's pad, the lined sheet had a numbered list of twenty in her surprisingly legible hand. Four of them we'd visited (and I'd touched) in the last week. Half a dozen more were in familiar towns. The rest, I hadn't the foggiest. Blyford? Hinderclay? Worlingham?

"Good work," I said. "There's twice as many on the real list… but this'll more than do until I – we – find it."

That look, again, with dad doing no more than keeping that little brain ticking over until her final year of astrophysics.

~~~~~~~

14

Next day, like Lola, Pevsner's wife, I was at the wheel once more. In the back, my mum and Eldest, naturally, but also Eldest's best mate. And, since I'd promised coffee and cake, my wife. To be fair, her day job concerns listed buildings so this recent thing of mine was a bit of a busman's holiday. That left Middler and The Boy back at the ranch, both of whom had better things to do.

"Have I got this right?" said Eldest's best mate. "We're off to see a wall?"

"Yeah," I said. "And?"

Westward Ho through Hintlesham and Hadleigh led us to Lovejoy land, aka Long Melford. Pevsner often includes a "perambulation" in larger towns. "Long Melford," he opines, "is long indeed".

Into the car park of the National Trust's very own **Melford Hall (#5)** where my wife flashed our membership cards at a pair of smiling volunteers.

"Visited before?" enquired the bearded gent.

"Not for a while," I said. "We're here to see the crinkle-crankle wall." In case that wasn't clear, I made the universal hand gesture of the snake. His mouth projected confusion.

"Nothing like that here," he said. Now my mouth mirrored his.

"Let's go," said my wife, stepping in before it all kicked off.

About to enter the hall itself, Eldest emitted an excited "Look!"

"That's what we've come to see?" said her best mate.

Wiggling into the garden was, of course, a wavy wall. Have to say it appeared relatively pristine and not very old. Then, having whizzed through the undoubted attractions of the house – Parker, porcelain, Potter – and out into the rear garden, we stumbled across the real McCoy. Easily taller than me, this gnarly wall includes a doorway. Historic England say it dates from 1793. Wow. That, of course, was the year of Marie-Antoinette's execution. To commemorate that, we all retreated into the scullery to eat cake.

With the late summer sun doing its utmost, it was now Eldest's turn to proclaim that we weren't yet done. She flashed her folded-up list at us.

"Oh, good," said my mum, gently glowing.

Half a mile's stroll back down that elasticated high street, just short of the Cock and Bell Inn, was a narrow walkway named **Cock and Bell Lane (#6, Long Melford)**. Our second catch of the day was another 8ft-tall vintage slithering stretch to our right. Had I been alone, I'd have joyfully rolled along its entire length in the last rays of the day.

Chapter 5

On the seventh day, like the beardy guy in the sky, we rested. A Sunday roast prepared by my wife – she could rest later – and a whole 24 hours for yours truly to bask as the featured author on the Paragraph Planet website. My micro-story *Like The Clappers* had, in my humble opinion, a beginning, a middle, and an end, all in 75 words. Why would you need more? The competition in that glossy magazine was ancient history.

I was enjoying some me-time loading the dishwasher, rinsing pans and listening to Kermode & Mayo's film reviews when Eldest had the misfortune to enter the kitchen.

"That list of walls" – I glanced sideways at the sacred scroll which clung magnetically to the fridge between Chop Suey House and Taj Mahal takeaway menus – "could you add a rough time to reach each one?"

She emitted air from her nostrils, a non-verbal cue which told me that she'd be happy to oblige in the near future. Sure enough she'd done that by the time I returned from work next day, bless her Pikachu socks. Which was why we were, like Canned Heat, On The Road Again.

~~~~~~~

Both daughters reclined in the freshly MOT-ed motor with, surprisingly, Eldest's Best Mate also along for the ride. She'd seen that brace of walls in Long Melford and now, like the rest of us dope fiends, she wanted more. Less surprisingly, my wife turned us down. Occupying the front seat was, of course, my mum.

Not sure what (if anything) you're thinking about a grown man (me!) spending quite so much time with his old ma. Cute? Cloying? Perfectly fine?

I evidently had a family of my own to look after. Admittedly the kids

17

needed less and less of my attention, and that was mostly fine with me. This recent spate of serpentine sightseeing was the most maternal contact I'd had in yonks.

Three years previously, in October 2012, my parents had celebrated their golden wedding anniversary with a bit of a do at the Orwell Hotel in Felixstowe: family and cake as far as the eye could see. Like us, they had their own lives to lead and were always out and about. We'd see them every other week, sometimes more often if my mum was acting as emergency babysitter or picker-upper, and that worked with everyone. Until, that is, my dad was rushed into hospital in Christmas 2014 and died a few weeks later. That was a tough time for all of us, especially my mum.

I'm not great at empathy – ask the cat – but it was upsetting to contemplate my mum at home, all alone. Hence, I guess, these trips that provided a great excuse to get out of the house, see something new, and socialise with people that she might like. Whenever one of my kids grazed a knee or fell off a bike, my favourite and perhaps only Practical Parenting technique was to distract them. Hey, do you see that funny-shaped cloud? Replace "cloud" with "wall" to bring us back to the present.

Leaving home, we'd set the controls for the postcode supplied by Eldest then sailed by Stonham Aspal and past Pettaugh. Official sunset, I'd noted, was 7:30pm on the dot. Not the best time to meet a nasty T-junction off the A1120. STOP, commanded the red and white octagon. Partly buried in the hedge opposite was a sign pointing right to Yoxford and Saxtead. Absolutely nothing was signed to the left.

"I don't think there's anything coming," said my mum, leaning forward and blocking my view. Ever helpful. We edged out. All quiet.

"Past this pub," said Eldest, indicating The Victoria, "then it's along here. May as well pull over by this verge." I duly stopped.

"Don't think I saw a name," I said, as Eldest and her mate walked off. "This is where?"

Middler pointed to a totemic structure standing in a newly mown grassy triangle. We wandered over. "Earl Soham, apparently. Where are they?" We scurried over to catch up with my mum. She in turn was trying to catch up with the girls.

"Here, somewhere," said Eldest. "I've seen this on Street View." That's my line, I thought. "Over there."

Beyond the white picket fence of **The Rookery (#7, Earl Soham)** sat a decent chunk of aged crinkle-crankle wall with perhaps half-a-dozen substantial bulges.

"That's a good one," observed Eldest's best mate, already an authority.

"Certainly is," I said, attempting to retain ownership of this venture.

Despite that, neither Pevsner nor the most recent 2010 Conservation Area Appraisal for Earl Soham deemed it worthy of a mention. Remains of something grander? Later I found out that Historic England had listed it as Grade II and described it as "30m long, 2.5m high and one brick thick."

"The night is young", I said, narrowing my eyes and trying to account for all passengers. "Any more nearby?"

"Well…," replied Eldest. She offered another IP postcode for me to bang in and off we drove through Dennington, everybody scanning the surroundings in case Mr Sheeran was out for a stroll. Ten minutes more took us into Yoxford town where, sure enough, the sun don't shine above the ground.

"There's meant to be one in there," said Eldest, pointing to the board for Satis House: hotel, restaurant, bar.

"We can't go in there," protested my mum.

"Course we can," said the driver, pulling in to the driveway. Me and the girls climbed out for a cursory look in the gloaming but to no avail.

"Enough excitement for one evening?" I turned to face the gang.

"There's one more site on the way home," suggested Eldest.

~~~~~~~

A Panorama special on Jeremy Corbyn's bid for the Labour leadership was about to start when we parked in the centre of Saxmundham. "In the main street," wrote Pevsner, "little need be noted." I'd disagree.

Walk north on **High Street (#8, Saxmundham)** past the town hall and The Bell and the chippy and the hardware shop to where the shops stop. You may well have driven this way yourself. Suddenly the wall to your left curves in and out and in and out as if pretending to lose its balance. This foolishness is briefly interrupted by the sensible straight edge of someone's house before the mock vertigo reasserts itself for another three bays. Those bricks don't seem hugely old and there's a distinctive black skirt along its length. Oddly, on close inspection, the wall comprises nothing but headers, i.e. the brick ends.

While my juvenile juveniles were doing their utmost to spoil my commemorative snaps – at least there was street lighting – a window opened upstairs in the sensible straight house. A woman leaned out and called down: "What are you doing?"

"Admiring this wall," I said, stroking the cool masonry and instantly becoming aware how crazed that both looked and sounded.

"That's my wall. Do you want a better view? You'll need to come round the other side."

"Um, thanks," I said automatically. "Round we go."

Waiting for us on Market Place was an open door. In we trooped, all five of us. A man, presumably the husband, said hello as if this type of thing happened all the time.

"This is the oldest house in the town," stated the woman. "And down there in my garden is another one of those walls." Everyone nodded. "Do you want to come upstairs?"

On the top floor, little need be noted … apart from the excessive number of dolls staring at us with their dead eyes from every shelf, ledge and cupboard. I glanced down at my wrist. Whenever I step in the back door from work, I remove my Casio timepiece.

"We really should be going," I spluttered. "Most kind. Thanks."

None of us looked back as we hurriedly returned to the parked car. Safely in our seatbelts and with that Saxmundham sign in the rear-view mirror, the giggling started.

Chapter 6

"Are you looking for something in our art, architecture & photography books store?" So began an alert from evil Amazon. Yes, Mr Bezos, I might well be interested in the first two – *Suffolk: East* and *Suffolk: West* by one James Bettley, hugely updated versions of Pevsner's original *Buildings of England* volume. Even with a welcome 20% off, however, they were still the best part of thirty quid each. Not now, ta.

The coming weekend happened to coincide with HODs, Heritage Open Days, when lots of usually private buildings throw open their doors to the great unwashed. Scanning Eldest's fridge list with my additional requested "time to reach" column, I paused at one near the bottom, 55 minutes away. A tad too far for a weekday post-tea peregrination; ideal for a Saturday saunter, especially since Mr Google had already informed me about some nearby HODs properties. Sorted.

~~~~~~~

Early Saturday afternoon, the sun had his hat on as the usual suspects and I sat outside my mum's house in the Whitehouse area of Ipswich. She'll tell you it's not actually Whitehouse but part of the High View estate, a name borrowed from the imaginatively titled High View Road nearby. She can back this up with an estate agent's letter from the early 1960s when my parents bought their place. Used to be all fields, you know. She opened the car door, a bigger smile on her face than usual and obviously keen to speak.

"Before we set off, I've made us all something."

She dug into her handbag and ceremoniously handed each of us a badge. A handmade, printed, plastic-sheathed rectangular badge complete with safety pin. Mine read:

Eldest had a big gold 2 by her name. Middler had 3, Eldest's best mate 4. The badges' creator had relegated herself to the number 5 slot.

"Thanks, Nana," piped the girls using that tone I'd taught them.

"I hope you'll be wearing these for today's outing," said my mum. The rear-view mirror offered a view of Middler slipping hers into the car door pocket, undoubtedly for safe-keeping. It worked. I found it there some years later.

Curiously our route north speared us through Bramfield (#2) – no stopping today – and on into unfamiliar Halesworth. Big day for the great and the good of the town, this being the first time they'd marked HODs. Perhaps previous attempts had been discouraged by Pevsner's casual observation: "There is nothing of special architectural interest in Halesworth." I saw that he hadn't included any reference to one of Norman Scarfe's walls. Still, Eldest's intel had been sound thus far.

We parked and, in the Market Place, we poked our heads into the foyer of a 1920s themed café called Tilly's. A passing man, presumably the proprietor, saw us gawping:

"Do you want to come upstairs?"

"Um, thanks," I said, totally forgetting the Saxmundham doll experience.

It was happening again. An impromptu and entertaining guided tour of his satisfyingly symmetrical building: amazing what happens when you show an interest. Afterwards we retired to the attached sun-drenched tea garden for coffee and cake.

"Come on, crew," I said, geeing them along. After all, I was now the official leader. I had a badge to prove it. "That wall isn't going to see itself."

We followed the Thoroughfare over the river, a leaflet for the Halesworth Town Trail held aloft, and veered left by the glass-fronted county library. Off Rectory Street leads a path marked Rectory Lane but known to locals as **Duck Lane (#9, Halesworth).** Catching the mid-afternoon dappled sunlight was a fine Grade II listed C18 serpentine wall, slightly taller than all of us, frustratingly. Doesn't everyone want to peek over? Less than five inches thick, according to Historic England, it includes a central gate and undulates pleasingly along the quiet lane.

"Another good one," remarked Eldest's best mate, aka crew member 4. We nodded, sagely.

~~~~~~~

Back home, that list gnawed away at me. I didn't doubt the solidity of the entries on Eldest's piece of paper – thanks, Tim Berners-Lee – yet her total of twenty walls fell well short of the tally claimed by Norman Scarfe. Why not go straight to the source? Answer: because, like my dad, Mr Scarfe had also joined the choir invisible. Had a good innings, did Norman, until his time ran out in 2014 aged four score years and ten.

Remember Mr Coulson who supposedly took over the list's upkeep? Among other roles, he'd been membership secretary of the SPS. Scottish Prison Service? Socialist Party of Serbia? No, the Suffolk Preservation Society: they're campaigning to protect the county I love, or so says their website. About time I dropped them a line:

"Hello there," I emailed. "I'm trying to find a list of crinkle-crankle walls in Suffolk." I made sure to namecheck Scarfe and Coulson and kept it brief.

"Unfortunately," came the speedy reply next morning, "I cannot find any mention of the survey you mention." Darn. Linda, their office manager, did however attach a scanned paragraph from Scarfe's *Shell Guide to Suffolk* in which he states:

"I once listed fifty-eight in the county."

But where, Norman, but where?

Reversing out of that particular cul-de-sac, I switched tack. On the soggy Sunday after our sunny Saturday in Halesworth, I'd had a rummage in the library of the Ipswich Institute. I chanced across a book by the

Suffolk Gardens Trust called Walled Gardens of Suffolk which included a reference to an article in their newsletter. The piece, written by "Martin, E.", had this intriguing title:

"Where are all the crinkle-crankle walls?"

Get me a copy of that and my itch would surely be scratched. Didn't take long to locate an email address for Mr Martin at Suffolk County Council and zing, off went another request. I was nearly there.

Except there was no response a day later, nor a week later. Nada. Nowt.

~~~~~~~

The following weekend, Eldest disappeared back to Welsh Wales for her third and final year at uni. A week later we took Middler to Bath for her first year at uni. That left me, my wife and The Boy. House: much quieter; bathroom access: much quicker.

Nine walls visited, eight of which I'd touched: that one at Earl Soham (#7) was out of reach. That appeared to be that. The crew had disbanded.

Chapter 7

From that first wall at Easton to the most recent example along Duck Lane had taken all of a fortnight. Now the serpentine charabanc had been garaged. Fun while it lasted.

Something that had lasted w-a-y longer was an entirely separate enterprise that I called "light lunches". At work among the boffins on the Brobdingnagian BT site at Martlesham Heath, three of us used to meet to eat: me, clearly, plus Andy, a charming Yorkshireman, and Grenvyle, a plain-speaking Lincoln City fan with poorly functioning kidneys.

We didn't share an office – none of us really knew what the other two did – but we'd instead bonded as members of one of the works' table tennis teams. Each of the ten or so teams was named for a type of plane that had flown from RAF Martlesham Heath, the land now occupied by a good chunk of the BT site. The Defiants, comprising we three plus a couple of others, were invariably to be found in the lower reaches of the Ipswich & District league. Grenvyle's bouts of poor health meant that he'd sometimes hold up his bat mid-rally then more or less collapse on to the table. Used to unnerve his opponent no end.

In a distant corner of the site stood a glorified portacabin containing two full-size snooker tables and two permanently set-up table tennis tables. We'd often rendezvous there for a half-hour knock before walking over to the central hub for our assorted packed lunches. As the weather hotted up, though, the ping-pong hut became stuffy so we'd ditch the sport of kings and head straight to the hub. No problem, except the conversation could flag towards the end of the working week. Then Andy had his 2007 brainwave: why not pop out to a nearby café for lunch at the end of the week? After all, genteel Woodbridge was only ten minutes' drive. We could be there and back in the allotted hour, give or take.

25

~~~~~~~

Our initial trip to The Wild Strawberry was a good 'un.

"You should write a review," suggested Andy as we lapped up the Market Hill sun that first week, "and stick it on your website."

"Guess I could," I heard myself say between bites on my really rather good crayfish & rocket sandwich.

Andy, always ambitious, then extended the idea to a summer tour. Every Friday, assuming we were all around, we'd tick off another place. Hence the Whistlestop, Caravan Café, Mrs Piper's, Notcutts, Pickwicks, Frangipani, etc. Within four months we'd exhausted Woodbridge: seventeen eateries visited, seventeen light lunches partaken, seventeen reviews posted. Must serve tea, must have seating, no restaurants, were the rough guidelines.

Did we stop there? Is that a rhetorical question? Felixstowe, five minutes further, kept us out of mischief for well over a year before we branched out to pick off Framlingham and other rural locations. After we unanimously agreed that we could all get away with a 90 minute lunch on a Friday, we started picking off the cafes in Ipswich. That coincided with cheery Roy Keane becoming manager of the once mighty ITFC.

We suffered quite a setback with Grenvyle's untimely death in 2010 – to be fair, he told us he was ill – but felt that we should carry on. His seat was filled by Kevin, a bat-wielding friend and Felixstowe poker shark.

Two days prior to that initial Easton crinkle-crankle excursion had seen a return trip to The Wild Strawberry for what Andy calculated was our 300th such outing. Their Pump Street sourdough sandwich with Creasey's bacon, tomato, and avocado was a thing of beauty. Grenvyle would have loved it.

It had become harder and harder to keep finding unvisited places within driving distance of work. All of us remained vigilant in our respective manors: Kevin on the coast, Andy in Woodbridge, me in Ipswich.

Thus it was that an email arrived in November 2015 from light lunch founder Andy saying:

"Just noticed the wavy wall behind the house. Is this on your list?"

Included was a link to somewhere called the Crockery Barn Café. Their web page had a photo of some classic cars lined up on the driveway and another showing an in-and-out brick wall. A muffled bell rung in my head: oh yeah, those things.

~~~~~~~

Early December – a Friday, naturally – our trio took Andy's range-limited and eerily silent electric Renault Zoe past the cafes at Wyevale (visited April 2008) and Grange Barn (June 2014) to Ashbocking, population 318. Behind the bedding plants in the stark winter sunlight stood the impressive 100 feet wall of the **Crockery Barn (#10, Ashbocking).** Had Eldest's best mate been there, she'd have nodded approvingly. Unlike all the previous examples I'd seen, this was nearly new; I hadn't appreciated that such structures were still being put up in the modern day. The website helpfully had the text of an article all about the wall published the previous year in the *Suffolk* magazine: isn't this where we came in?

Built by one David Starling over six weeks, it had been commissioned in 1999 by the Sargent family to replace a nondescript breezeblock structure. Such walls, the article said:

"…were usually built by wealthy land owners to use up the many bricks left over after building stately homes."

I'd not heard that one before. As I snapped away at various arty angles with my phone, Kevin remarked:

"These are the things you travel miles to see?"

Our trio retreated into the Barn itself for bacon & mushrooms on toast, pumpkin soup with cheese scone, and a turkey & cranberry sandwich. All very Christmassy.

~~~~~~~

Talking of which, we soon had a houseful again with the festive return of

27

the undergrads. Bang went the bathroom. Boxing Day been and gone, the family was stuck in Crimbo Limbo and desperate for an excuse to get out in the fresh air. Eldest and I looked at each other in the kitchen and both stared at the fridge list, untouched since September.

"You text Nana," I said, "and find out if she's free."

It was agreed that The Boy could guard the house on condition that it didn't burn down. Eldest's best mate wasn't around – shame – but Middler's best mate was, and in possession of a driving licence and an MOT-ed car.

"Tell you what," I told Middler, "we'll pick up Nana and meet you at The Shed. Keep your phone on."

In my role as king of the cafeterias, I'd done some Googling and found a recommended place at Henstead. No, me neither, but it was en route to our intended destination. We were a few miles away when my phone buzzed:

"The Shed. It's closed. Opens again in January."

"Typical," added my wife.

We agreed to carry on into Beccles and found spots at the free car park down by the riverside.

"That place is meant to be good," I said, pointing to The Quay café.

"Also closed," observed my wife. Come to Beccles, expect heckles.

My prayers were answered when we spotted some lights in The Garden Tea Rooms. Table for six? No problem. Better still, they were still serving hot food and of the no-nonsense kind favoured by my mum. I recalled an unhappy incident at a swish eatery with some giant cous-cous.

Other folk had clearly felt the same need for a change of scenery. Scanning the room, I nudged my mum:

"Isn't that…?"

"It is!" she said, and got up to walk over to another table. There sat a couple that she'd known for years and years until they'd moved away from Ipswich. Tony, the grey-haired gent, had been kind enough to say a few words at my dad's funeral. Top man. How odd to bump into them. Of all the tea rooms in all the towns in all the world. I took it as a good sign.

~~~~~~~

The day was getting away from us by the time we finally walked out of TGTR. That didn't matter. We were fed.

"Round here," said Eldest, turning a corner. Near the delightfully named Puddingmoor was the ever narrowing **Hungate Lane (#11, Beccles),** home to a well weathered slab of Grade II listed crinkle-crankle, apparently part of Homefield House once upon a time. My mum and I pulled out our phones.

Middler's best mate addressed Middler: "This is what we've come to see?"

Everybody returned to their respective motors for a five minute drive to the outskirts of Beccles. Through an unremarkable 60s estate runs Coney Hill, weirdly, as my mum recalled, home to the friends she'd just been chatting to in the team room. At its intersection with **Bluebell Way (#12, Beccles)** winds a long piece of modern serpentine. There were too many bays to count in the failing light. With a similar black skirt to Saxmundham, it probably predates Ashbocking by ten or twenty years. Nice place to catch your bus into town.

Eldest then proclaimed that we weren't yet done, demonstrating that maxim about the apple and the tree.

Totally guided by the satnav we edged out of Beccles, beam on, to enter the parish of Worlingham. Up here, somewhere, was **Garden Lane (#13, Worlingham)**. We parked and wandered up and down until we finally found it, a 40m length of listed and looming crinkle-crankle. Robert Wadlow, tallest ever man, measured 2.7m. He would not have been able to peek over the top since this remarkable red brick relic stands a full 3.5m tall. Not ideal viewing conditions at quarter-to-five on a chilly December afternoon, but hey.

Thus ended 2015, annus sinuous.

~ 2016 ~

Chapter 8

My extramural studies recommenced two days into the New Year:

> *"We thought you'd like to know that your Dodo Wall Pad 2016 order has been dispatched."*

Said pad described itself as "a combined family diary doodle memo message engagement organiser calendar" and had proved invaluable in previous years for plotting our familial comings and goings. If it's not on the pad, it's not happening. Its value had dropped now that the girls' entries contained little more than university term dates.

~~~~~~~

Revitalised by the reassembly of the crew for that Beccles constitutional, I'd re-Googled a certain name and got a hit. So, back at my desk on the first Monday of the year, and finding some free time before lunch, I knocked off a quick email to the Suffolk Institute of Archaeology and History, as you do:

> *"I'm trying to contact Edward Martin about crinkle-crankle walls in Suffolk. I believe he's written at least one article about them and I'd like to get a copy."*

Nothing of consequence nestled in my inbox after my strict 60 minute break, but my prior email to his Suffolk County Council address had similarly yielded nowt. This time I'd clicked my heels and spun around in my chair before hitting "send". Like I tell the kids, you've gotta want it.

Sure enough, next morning came a reply from some kind SIAH soul to say they'd forwarded my message. Ten-thirty on the dot arrived an email from none other than Edward Martin, BA, FSA, MifA. He attached a copy of that mythical article for which I'd been searching, entitled *"Where are all the crinkle-crankle walls?"* I breathed in and scrolled down, keen to finally discover the answer posed by the article's title and to maybe draw a line under this minor obsession.

In two paragraphs it became clear that Edward and I not only shared regal nomenclature but that we'd been cruising on the same dual carriage-way. His article mentioned Easton (#1), Eye (#3) and Halesworth (#9), namechecked Norman Scarfe and G.A. Coulson, and concluded:

> *"The whereabouts of the [Scarfe/Coulson] list is, unfortunately, unknown to Norman, to the Suffolk Record Office, the Suffolk Preservation Society and the archaeological service of Suffolk County Council. Does anyone know where a copy may be found?"*

"Oh," I uttered.

"Something up?" said a colleague.

"No, not really." We returned to our respective screens.

Of the eight walls cited in his article, the crew had visited half. Perhaps we could combine resources to form a crinkle-crankle catamaran? After all, two Eds are better than one. I sent him a list of the thirteen we'd seen and another twelve or so on the to-do list.

Once Broom Acres was quiet that evening, I grabbed Eldest's list from the grip of its tenacious steel fridge magnet and placed it by my keyboard. This won't take long, I thought. Somewhat later, after a hot chocolate, two rounds of toast and a mug of PG's finest, I dragged myself up the wooden hill to Bedfordshire. There on my website for everyone to read – my mum, certainly – was a blog post with the clickbait title *"Crinkle-crankle walls of Suffolk"*. In the introductory waffle I named Pevsner, Scarfe, Coulson and Edward Martin, my new learned friend, and described the baker's dozen of sightings to date, each accompanied by one of my choice snaps. A bunch of these, I realised, had been taken in near darkness, such as blacked out Brome Grange (#4) and the shadowy monster of Worlingham (#13). For my own use, the post ended with a list of those as yet unseen. That section seemed like a statement of intent.

~~~~~~~

Wasn't at my most productive in the office the morning after the night before. Yet, aided by a mid-morning jolt of Taylor's Rich Italian, I felt pretty pleased with my endeavours,. There used to be a list – that list vanished – and now I'd created a new list. Cocky and caffeinated, I took to the Twitter:

> *(1/4) Hey, people of Suffolk, did you know we have the most crinkle-crankle walls in the country? #crinklecrankle*
> *(2/4) Crinkle-crankle walls are those curvy brick constructions like the really long one at Easton. #crinklecrankle*
> *(3/4) There are others at Beccles, Bramfield, Eye, Halesworth, etc, and maybe 50 or more in total. #crinklecrankle*
> *(4/4) Here are the ones I know about -- tinyurl.com/crinklecrankle -- can you add to the list? Suffolk only, please. Thanks! #crinklecrankle*

How do you like that hashtag?

Those tweets procured some likes, provoked some retweets and produced some replies: had I seen the one at Eye? Did I know about the one opposite Bramfield church? Yes to all of the above.

Undaunted, and aware that different people are on the Twitter at different times of day, I put out a similar Coulson-esque appeal eight hours later during something called Suffolk hour. More replies: isn't there a crinkle-crankle wall at Orford? How about that one on the A134? Was I aware of Tostock Place? Clearly there's a more informed crowd on social media of an evening.

Not only that but the man with two first names, Edward Martin, had replied again:

"My list has now risen to 57 and here is a selection that you can perhaps add to your 'to see' list:

His "selection" ran to 21 lines and covered half of the alphabet from Alderton to Wattisfield. Having merged those and my handful of Twitter leads into the to-do bit of my page, that total easily dwarfed those already seen. A number of them seemed to be located at halls. The majority of place names meant nothing to me. Both daughters were about to return to their remote studies. I felt the candle of my confidence flicker and dim.

~~~~~~~

Nonetheless, the show must go on. Crew members 1 and 5 – my mum and I – polished our badges and reported for duty that Saturday afternoon. Not hot, not cold, with no discernible colour in the sky.

"No girls?" she said, fumbling with her seatbelt.

"Gone!"

"Oh, OK. I saw your website," she continued. "So there's still another ten or so wibbly-wobbly walls to track down?"

"Ah, that was midweek," I said. "Lot's happened since then. Let me fix that belt and I'll tell you."

Given the wealth of walls from which to pick, I'd opted for one about half an hour's drive away. We retraced our route that we'd taken four months previously to Long Melford (#5 and #6) along the A1071. After an intriguing sign to Calais Street – how did that name come to be? – we turned off into Boxford. Ex-wool town, home of Copella apple juice, it's quintessential Suffolk with dainty cottages lined along the river Box.

Let's pause to take in the regulation village sign: church, tree, windmill, watermill, corn, apples, and a lion lounging in a motorcycle sidecar. That would be due to George "Tornado" Smith, son of the White Hart landlord.

In the late 1920s he was famed for bringing the wall of death (now that's a wall I'd like to have seen) to this country. Sometimes he was joined by Marjorie Dare – his wife – and later by Briton, his very own lioness. They say that Briton was buried in the pub's car park.

"OK," I said, "Edward Martin BA says there's a wall on Church Street."

My mum swivelled her head. "Well, there's the church." Together we're a crack team.

"So I see. Earliest timber porch in the county, they say."

I didn't mention that I'd borrowed that factoid from Pevsner. He'd seen fit to admire "a pretty row of timber-framed houses" on Church Street. Up and down we perambulated. Those historical properties stood arm-in-arm, presenting an impenetrable Siegfried Line. With no friendly constable to ask, we entered the village shop, the Boxford Stores, not to be confused with the Village Stores directly opposite. I placed a pack of Trebor Softmints on the counter, the token required to pose my question. To his credit, the shopkeeper didn't flinch.

"That wavy wall," said the helpful chap, "is behind the orange house. Not visible from the road. Though it can be seen."

"How?"

"From the top of the church…" – we both glanced out of the window – "which is only open in the summer." He shrugged. "That'll be 60p, please."

This was new: we weren't accustomed to defeat. Outside, with fresh breath confidence, we cut down a driveway leading to the village surgery. Being set back, its position afforded us a sneaky view of the rear gardens.

"Over there!"

We wandered across an open green area to behold a fabulously knobbly and awfully curvy old crinkle-crankle wall behind **Church Street (#14, Boxford)**. I stroked the brickwork and imagined Tornado Smith revving his engine while considering whether to take on this weird wall, which skirted round a corner to disappear from sight. As did we before the local bobby spotted us. Good view of the church tower, by the way. Twenty past three on an overcast Saturday and the candle burned bright.

35

Naturally we weren't yet done. We're never done. Fifteen minutes later we'd reparked in Sudbury and were strolling along Friars Street away from the town centre.

"In there?" asked my mum, checking out The Strawberry Teacake.

"Love to, but later. We've got work to do."

"If you say so. And this other one's along here according to this Edward bloke?"

"Apparently."

"Nice name." She paused. "But you don't know where exactly?"

I shook my head. Friars Street, we discovered, runs and runs like Brendan Foster. Many period properties, the odd ordinary wall, but no obvious serpentine. The shops stopped. Time to consult someone from Sudbury itself. One family group wouldn't catch my eye – put yourself in their shoes – but a chap on the far side of the road foolishly did. Grey anorak and green carrier bag, he took my question on the chin:

"Crinkle-crankle? Yes, I know it. It's where I work. And we've got a folly in the garden too. I can go that way into town. Care to follow me?"

Oh lord, I thought, we've got a right one here. Best go with it. We marched in time to the pendulum of his carrier bag, nipping through an alleyway – "Bullocks Lane," he commented – to emerge into Meadow Lane.

"Here," he said. "This is **The Red House (#15, Sudbury)**. I'll leave you here if that's OK. Must catch the shops before they close." And our Sudbury Samaritan had gone.

"Nice man," said my mum. "Ooh, that's a lot of ins and outs."

Taller than me and beginning with a short straight section, as if finding its feet, the wall became a sine wave, on and on and on. A double-yellow line along its length seemed hopelessly square by comparison. Both this stretch on Meadow Lane and its continuation into Red House Lane are Grade II listed. These days, The Red House ("the stateliest Georgian house in Sudbury", according to Pevsner) is a care home. Its name dates back to the 18th century and assorted mayors of the town have called it home. One of these, Joseph Humphrey, is thought to have had the curvy walls added. And while there was no constable in Boxford, it's believed that Gainsborough lived here once. That would have been years prior to the crinkle-crankles. Oh, and the folly mentioned by our steersman turned out to be a 200-year-old gazebo that sits in the grounds.

After a brace of hard-to-find examples, we were more than deserving of refreshments at thankfully-still-open David's café. We want cake and tea! A most satisfying day.

Chapter 9

Next morning found me sweating in a sports hall, racket in hand. Me and The Boy faced off at badminton every Sunday against another father/son combo. Used to be that the dads did all the running around at the back with the boys picking up the odd net shot. Nowadays our offspring were the ones smashing that feathery projectile past our ageing ears, or occasionally square into the spine.

Home for a double shot Nespresso, a hot shower and then to write up the previous day's visits with a tip of the hat to both Edward Martin and the green carrier bag man. The to-do list appeared undiminished. Minus the girls, the three of us enjoyed a subdued roast.

"Are you finally going to take those bags to the dump after lunch or are you off to see yet more walls?" enquired my wife.

~~~~~~~

Early afternoon and I was perspiring again. I'd lugged four fertiliser sacks of crazy paving fragments into the boot and thence to the tip. My load was lighter in all ways. As may be evident, if I'm out in the car I like to kill multiple birds. I rechecked the postcode on my little sheet before typing it in. Surely CO is Colchester?

Wherstead and Tattingstone whizzed past before a board for "afternoon teas at Rose Cottage" snagged my eye. Must mention that to the light lunch chaps. The road bent right near The Bull as I entered Brantham.

"Make a U-turn," advised the patient satnav woman. Oops, missed it. Planning ahead, I'd observed that Street View offered no foretaste of my destination. Maybe the driver had also missed that turn-off.

"Make a U-turn," she repeated, remarkably calmly.

"I'm trying!"

That bit of the A137 is fast. A handy layby came and went on the wrong side. Eventually, nearing Essex, I used a roundabout to slingshot back.

Turning into Newmill Lane, holding up the traffic in both directions, is nasty. You're funnelled into a narrow track and, like some lo-res Atari game, must guide your wheels along parallel paths while keeping the grassy midriff aligned with your gearstick. Fields to the right of me, fields to the left of me, then behold **Seafield House (#16, Brantham)**.

There's a super useful website called Geograph with the tagline "photograph every grid square". Fortunately for me, one Keith Evans had visited this very spot three years earlier and uploaded his image of a "crinkle-crankle wall near to Brantham, Suffolk". And it's a doozy, comprising nine or so bays, each around 25 bricks tall, that recede into the middle ground as it they might go on for ever. A few days later I exchanged messages with Ed Keeble, talented local bird artist, who told me that his parents had the wall built around 1960. They'd been inspired by the Eye specimen at Chandos Lodge (#3) and had also taken a good look at Easton (#1) before laying down the footprint with cedar frames. Those are gone – woodworm – but his parents still have photos of its construction.

I didn't hang around long lest any other vehicle require access to the lane, and headed straight home. Not really: I had one more location to scout.

~~~~~~~

Eldest – remember her? – had identified a wriggler twenty minutes from here. I waved in the rough direction of Griff Rhys Jones in Stutton, saluted myself when passing the Royal Hospital School, and puzzled over the proper peninsula pronunciation of Chelmondiston. End of the line here is Shotley. Actually it's the linked village of Shotley Gate with its fine views of Harwich over the water in darkest Essex. Shotley, claimed firstborn, had a crinkle-crankle wall in The Street. In spite of some late morning Googling, that was the extent of my knowledge.

Around 3pm I parked by the purple Premier stores – they'd shut their doors an hour earlier – and paraded along The Street (upper or lower case is acceptable). Nothing, nada, nix. Hopping back in the motor, I coasted along to the peninsula's Land's End at Shotley Gate. Not a takeaway coffee to be had. Not even a Costa, and they're everywhere.

Perhaps she'd been having me on? I retraced my route and reclaimed my Premier parking place – still shut – and expended some more shoe leather. This was a dank Sunday afternoon in early January and I badly needed to be sitting down with a cuppa and a slice of something sugary. About to give up, I saw the elusive structure, right there on **The Street (#17, Shotley)**.

Waist-high, it snaked from the road to the front of a pair of houses, separating the driveway on the left from the garden on the right, and was maybe a dozen bricks tall with red reflectors on the roadside pillar. As Stephen Fry used to say in an old building society advert, it's compact and bijou and therefore easy to miss. Wall nabbed, I hit "home" on the satnav. Seriously.

~~~~~~~

Thinking of going to bed that evening, I saw a message from Radio Suffolk's very own Lesley Dolphin. To my "Can you add to this list?" tweet, she'd replied:

"Why do you want to know?"

I tweeted back, quicksnap:

"Suffolk has the most crinkle-crankle walls but nobody has a definitive list. It's become a quest to identify and visit them!"

I reread what I'd written. My fate was sealed. I had a quest.

Chapter 10

The second Monday of 2016 was a big day. You might well remember it. I was invited to appear on BBC local radio; two MPs got in touch; oh, and the world woke up to discover that David Bowie had died.

Explaining my quest to Lesley Dolphin had prompted an email exchange with Radio Suffolk.

Lesley would like to broadcast your appeal tomorrow afternoon: would that be alright?
Great, thanks.
Would you be free to come in to the studio?
Not really, since I work full time.
Could we talk to you on the phone instead?
Yes, I guess so.
OK, let's say 2:30pm.

That evening Lesley Dolphin tweeted to her 10,000 followers:

So where are Suffolk's crinkle-crankle walls? We're making a list @BBCSuffolk on Tuesday afternoon.

Handily for me, she'd quoted my own tweet about the lack of a list, meaning that we'd both see the replies. Within half an hour of those Dolphin clicks and whistles came an unexpected notification: *"Therese Coffey mentioned you."*

Gosh. Therese Coffey. Conservative member of parliament for Suffolk Coastal, successor to John "Burger" Gummer. Deputy leader of the House of Commons. Close friends get to call her TC.

43

She'd sent me a link to a recent auction run by Clarke and Simpson. Lot 41 was described as "oil on board, *'Crinkle Crankle Wall To The Vineyard At Sibton, Spring 1982'* by one John Andrew Bawtree. Five minutes Googling told me that Sibton was 10 minutes north of Saxmundham but little else. "Don't suppose you know where that vineyard might be?" I tweeted back, not really expecting an answer. "Maybe Sibton Park or abbey," she replied. I took it all back.

Ping! Another curious notification: *"Dr Dan Poulter mentioned you. "*

Heck. Dan Poulter. Conservative member of parliament for Central Suffolk and North Ipswich, successor to Michael "Baron Framlingham" Lord. I'd once been in a Costa Coffee (Ipswich, not Shotley) with my mum when she pointed out someone ahead of us in the queue. "That's Dr Dan," she whispered. I swear she swooned.

Anyway, Poulter's prognosis was that "probably the best example is in Easton." Easton? I, I can remember standing by the wall. With ten minutes left of the day, I replied: "Thanks, but no points for naming Easton. That's the one everybody knows." I heard nothing more from the good doctor.

Showered and shaved and sweetly smelling next day, I tweeted about my imminent appearance on the Beeb:

I'll be on @BBCSuffolk this pm with @lesleydolphin talking crinkle-crankle walls. Can you add to my current list?

To which Eldest, nearly 300 miles away on the far side of Offa's Dyke, responded: "Are you being serious? This is amazing. PS stop visiting them without me."

I must have left my desk at one because I always do. Over a Tesco meal deal, Andy and Kev provided some intensive media training: think before you speak, talk with confidence even if you don't know what you're talking about, and here's a selection of words not to use on live radio.

Back to the office to read a couple of emails, then I nonchalantly picked up my Oxford Black & Red notebook, exited the main open plan area and sat myself in our functionally titled Small Meeting Room as if about to give or receive a quarterly appraisal. Over the last three months, Ed, can you give me two examples of how you've met your KPIs?

Before I could answer, my xylophone ringtone fired into life.

"Hi, Ed. Radio Suffolk here. We're going to put you on air in the next few minutes. Please stand by."

I cleared my throat, brushed a hand through my hair and felt a clamminess on the back of my neck. Then I cleared my throat again: should have brought a bottle of water, idiot.

"...and on the line to tell us all about these crinkly-crankly walls is Ed from Ipswich. Ed, how did you become interested in these wobbly walls?"

Blah blah Suffolk magazine blah blah Easton blah blah Norman Scarfe...

What felt like three hours' wittering was over in fifteen minutes. Still clutching my notebook, I sashayed into the office and reclaimed my seat while doing my damnedest not to catch anybody's eye. "Chris," I said to my colleague, "did you find those files I was after?" Attack is the best form of defence.

My number one priority during the interview had been to appeal to Lesley's legions of listeners for more locations. No, that isn't true. It was to not make a fool of myself. I thought it went swimmingly but had no intention of listening to it ever again: is there anyone who likes the sound of their own voice apart from, perhaps, your local MP?

As hoped for, more tweets came my way: some intriguing new suggestions such as Great Waldingfield and Rendlesham; some that technically weren't in the county of Suffolk, such as Yeldham in Essex; and others that would require some teasing out. For example:

[Jimmy] There is one between Cavendish and Clare on the A1092.
[me after Googling] That's a 2 mile stretch! Can you be any more specific, please?
[Jimmy] Sorry, I've just remembered that's not crinkle-crankle. Memory is going.

Hats off to the lovely Lesley Dolphin for indulging my quest. Not only was she good enough to drop me a line later saying that "it made great radio" – ahem – but she compiled a l-o-n-g list of listener suggestions. Peter in Melton, Brenda in Acton, Derek in Felixstowe and many other folk had all felt compelled to contact BBC Suffolk. It's very easy to be snooty about the Alan Partridge aspects but this was local radio in full effect.

Chapter 11

I've mentioned in passing that my wife's interest in this enterprise was just that: passing. Being a building conservationist for a local authority, her working hours are expended trying to protect old piles of bricks. Off duty, then, she didn't need me, still basking in my Radio Suffolk afterglow, to bang on about a 200-year-old wall in Wickham Market.

"You do know," she said over a reduced family tea with The Boy, "that you can search Historic England's site for listed buildings? Including any walls?"

"Right," I said. Meaning no, I didn't.

She sampled a spoonful of chicken curry; it had been my turn to cook. "Did you put any salt in this?"

"Search the list" is the online invitation extended by Historic England: scheduled monuments, battlefields, protected wrecks, you name it. Their advanced search lets you limit the results to a county – e.g. Suffolk – with your choice of keyword – e.g. crinkle-crankle. I clicked the blue search button: boom, 18 results. A smattering of familiar names (Cock and Bell Lane, Chandos Lodge) was submerged by a jungle of exotic locations (Cockfield, Rickinghall Inferior, etc.). I retried with "serpentine": boom, 43 results. Top of this apparently random pile, maybe based on syllable count, was Heveningham Hall.

I sent myself both lists: they hit my inbox like two interlocking halves of a giant boulder. Once more I sensed the weight of this entirely self-imposed Sisyphean task. Biking home, I vowed to not use the "w" word that evening. We talked about The Boy's day at school – fine – and any glimpses of the girls on social media since, naturally, neither had been in touch.

47

Come 9pm, dishwasher prepped, coffee poured, The Boy merrily dispatching the undead in the front room, we bookended the back room sofa. In the first ad break of Deutschland 83, a drama set six years prior to the fall of the Berlin unmentionable, my wife piped up:

"Oh, forgot to bring it up but Jason at work says there's a crinkle-crankle wall at Martlesham…"

I fumbled among the remotes, stabbed the pause button and gestured for her to elucidate. Two minutes later, data transfer complete, we resumed the gripping Germanic tale.

~~~~~~~

Most of the former RAF Martlesham is no more, a sizeable chunk of it under BT's Adastral Park, my place of work. Remnants of the RAF runway were popular for learner drivers. Somehow the control tower has survived; it now operates as an aviation museum. I cycle past it most days before emerging on to Eagle Way, a horseshoe that twists and turns from one A12 roundabout (Tesco) to the next (BT). The morning after our Deutschland discussion, I took a minor detour in Martlesham Heath. Sometimes it's good to spread your wings on the breeze. At a steady 5mph I scanned left and right using my Action Man patented Eagle Eyes (operated by moving a lever at the back of the neck). Side road, no; driveway, no; wooden fence, no; curvy wall, yes!

Here on **Eagle Way (#18, Martlesham Heath)** was a short salmon-pink stretch of serpentine brickwork, clearly contemporary and a soupcon more weathered than Ashbocking (#10). Dark bark chips filled both recesses. I waited for a female dogwalker to pass before kneeling down to take a photo. The Labrador turned its head to query my behaviour.

As delighted as I was to find it, I thought the wall had no good reason to be there. None of this estate existed when Pevsner toured Suffolk. In his 2015 updated Pevsner volume, James Bettley names Feilden & Mawson as the 1980s architects of this development and cites this very wall as one of the area's "neo-vernacular features". Fancy!

Much obliged to Jason. We should form a support group, those of us with quests.

~~~~~~~

At work I discreetly checked my Gmail to discover that my radio appeal continued to resonate: I'd acquired a Smiley-esque network of agents in various Suffolk towns, complimented by improbably named informants (I give you Worzel in Dunwich) ready to rat on their own neighbourhoods.

That Friday I suggested to Andy that we could shoot two birds by taking in a wall en route to a light lunch. Half an hour's eco-driving in his Zoe took us to Yoxford, the last village in Pevsner's *Buildings of England: Suffolk*. His penultimate paragraph reads:

> (SATIS HOUSE. In the garden an undulating or crinkle-crankle
> wall. N. Scarfe)

Andy indicated left and we coasted noiselessly into the grounds of the aforementioned house, now a "boutique restaurant". You may remember that the crew came here before but departed empty-handed due to the darkness – the light levels, not the Lowestoft lads. This time, a youth working in reception was as helpful as he could be to the quizzical gent standing before him. Back out in the driveway he pointed to a gently curving low wall in the driveway of **Satis House (#19, Yoxford)**.

"Maybe this?"

"I guess so," was the best I could muster. Barely a dozen bricks tall, it didn't seem as if it would merit acknowledgment from Norman Scarfe. It was, however, undeniably undulating. Perhaps there was a grander example round the back or the old one had been rebuilt? The accosted receptionist couldn't comment.

Less than five minutes away was Sibton, the village cited by Therese

Coffey MP. That Bawtree painting depicted a vineyard: on a slow drive past the church with a distant view of the abbey, there was nothing but the futuristic whine of his electric car. Best left for another time since our bellies were calling to us.

We were in Peasenhall before we knew it and parked outside the distinctive blue and gold frontage of Emmett's, posh deli and allegedly "the oldest artisan ham and bacon producer in the UK". Their café must be quiet in the New Year since they were offering an all-day breakfast deal for £2.16. Four coins? Don't mind if we do. Quality bacon, quality banana chutney, plus a decent cuppa thrown in. Tracking down walls has its pleasures, to be sure, but that full English would have satisfied Mick & Keith.

Chapter 12

Two weeks had flowed by since Ma and I had last gone crinkle-crankling. I'd had a few solo outings and, after the fact, updated her with my findings. She accepted that with good grace even though I sensed she'd rather have seen them too. To keep her wall-eye in, she told me, she'd extended her drive after picking up her grandson (my nephew) in order to take in that 1980s example at Martlesham Heath (#18). Every new sighting, she posted on Facebook; I did the same on Twitter. The online world has as many platforms as Crewe station.

An email from my learned friend Edward Martin arrived to acknowledge my website – the closest thing to a published list of Suffolk's crinkle-crankle walls – and to clarify some locations. For once I was happy not to be adding to the to-do list which had sprouted like leylandii since my various appeals and now required attention. A dry weekend beckoned and my mum was more than up for a trip.

"Will be round at 12:15," I texted.

"See you at 12:30," she batted back.

I pulled into the kerb alongside my childhood home at half-twelve exactly. A regal hand waved through the net curtain. Psyched to spot some unseen serpentines, a fistful of postcodes in my pocket, I watched two figures approach the Qashqai.

"Afternoon," said my mum. "OK if your nephew joins us?"

"Hey, nephew." He flashed a small laminated card at me like a commuter with a season ticket.

"Nana made me a badge. She said I had to bring it."

Crinkle-crankle crew member 6. That noise emitted from my mouth was the very definition of a harrumph.

"In my day you had to earn one of those. Anyway, welcome to the

51

crew. Long time no see."

His innocent features expressed some confusion. "But you were at my birthday party last week?"

"And that," I said, "is the joke."

For his tenth birthday, all available family members had donned multiple layers – this was mid-January – and converged on the Ipswich Model Engineering Society. That boy was loco for locos, and the IMES boasted an actual ride-on railway. My mum had arranged this, plus cake in the clubhouse. She's good like that.

"Can't promise many trains today," I told him. "But we should be seeing lots of wavy walls. Can you keep count for me, please?"

"Sure. When are we having lunch?"

Our route writhed through unfamiliar villages. Nedging Tye and Monks Eleigh gave way to Little Waldingfield, which was great but we needed Great Waldingfield. Left at a T-junction before a handily placed grassy triangle enabled us to pull over and get our bearings.

"Over there!" exclaimed a young voice.

"Thank you, number 6."

Our older eyes followed his finger to quite a length of crinkle-crankle set back from the road. I'd been told about this section at **Babergh Place Farm (#20, Great Waldingfield)** by, deep breath, Su Harris and Hilary Drain and Roy Connelly and Pat Bridges and Brenda in Acton. Mighty and majestic yet unlisted, it stands twenty or so bricks tall with obvious signs of repair.

[In March 2020 it would appear in the East Anglian Daily Times when two sections collapsed after a storm:

"The crinkle-crankle wall in Great Waldingfield is believed to be around 200 years old and one of only a handful in the county."

A handful?!

Later that year, in October 2020, Historic England announced that the wall, "likely to have been built in the 1840s," was now Grade II listed.]

That wall used to form part of the garden of Babergh Place, which, like the Electric Banana in Spinal Tap, is "not there any more". I was slightly miffed at being unable to touch those ancient bricks. If you have an idle minute, let me commend the satellite view to you.

"How many's that?" I asked as we picked up speed.

"Um, one?"

"Give the boy a coconut!"

"I don't want a coconut. I want some lunch!"

"Can you hang on a bit longer?" asked his grandmother. "Though I'm getting peckish too," she added sotto voce.

The B1115 guided us to a sweet spot on Gainsborough Street by Gainsborough's House in Gainsborough's home town of Sudbury. I wasn't to know that it would take us past McDonald's. As I herded them away from the town centre, there was growing dissent in the ranks. Much grumbling, stomachs rumbling.

"You got given that badge but you've got to earn that food," I said.

With its projecting upper storeys embellished by monochrome circles and stripes, Hardwicke House has been sitting on busy Stour Street for over 300 years. Senior Sudburyians might just remember it as the Sudbury Secondary School for Girls. Nowadays it's a doctor's surgery. Which, at 1:30pm on a Saturday, was closed. However, to the left of the locked gates was a low (straight) wall.

"Won't be a minute," I said, and nipped over before my mum could persuade me otherwise. At the very back of the car park is, you guessed it, a wavy wall belonging to **Hardwicke House (#21, Sudbury)**: some parts old-ish, some new-ish. Unremarkable, to be honest, and not the most attractive setting although the bricked up doorway is a curio. Huge tip of the hat to local snapper Tim Ranson for not only alerting me to this one but also providing photographic proof.

"OK?" I said, returning to my nonplussed companions who'd remained on the pavement throughout. What kind of example was I setting? "We'll go back a different way into town, then we'll eat, deffo."

My recent email exchange with Edward Martin had concerned a wall that may or may not exist on nearby Friars Street. After much unsatisfactory Googling, I'd decided to go straight to the top by bothering the chairman

(and founder) of the Sudbury History Society. He'd written the book —
several, actually — on the town. His name? Barry Wall. I kid you not.

Mr Wall was of maximum help on the landline. Better still, a rarity in
this quest, he could be definitive:

"There are three crinkle-crankle walls here in town," he told me. "The
Red House" — which we'd seen last time (#15) — "Hardwicke House, and
Christopher Lane." Referring to the Red House, he alluded to some recent
personal research. "Wish I could say more," he said, keeping me guessing.

In turn, I'd passed on these nuggets to my Twitter buddy Tim; he'd
then strolled into town and taken more snaps. One of my best agents, that
Tim. However, I needed to see it myself, and so guided our ravenous trio
down School Street and into what Tim called Crissy Lane.

"Behind there," observed my nephew with no exclamation mark,
nodding to **Grammar School Place (#22, Sudbury)**. "That's three today.
Can we eat, please?"

A goodly part of this one is obscured by flower beds and foliage. I like
to think that if the local schoolgirls had their wall at Hardwicke House,
then the local schoolboys had theirs here as part of the venerable Sudbury
Boys Grammar School. Attended in the late 1730s, naturally, by Thomas
Gainsborough himself, William Wood House, site of the old school and
dating back to 1491, is now, like The Red House, a care home. Such is
the fate of huge hard-to-maintain houses. Photos were taken and off we
marched in search of sustenance.

Left into Friars Street and my mum pointed out someone walking away
from the town centre. Remember the chap who helped us out on this very
street, green carrier bag man? I stopped him to convey my thanks and to
update him on the Sudbury serpentine count.

"That's good," he said. "I saw your thing on Twitter." And we said our
goodbyes once again.

David's Café had worked well for us on our previous visit. About to
go in, my mum noticed a sign on the door: *No Children*. Wow. "Nobody
panic," I said, panicking and rapidly scanning shop fronts. "Let's try over
there."

54

Thank goodness for the no-frills Coffee House – love that Ronseal name – and their all day breakfasts. We'd have lingered longer had the staff not been putting chairs on tables all around us. Unlike us, their day was done.

"Right. Everybody ready for one more stop?" My mum's mug of tea and my nephew's Fruit Shoot hung in mid-air.

"Seriously?" said the mug of tea.

"We're not going to walk, are we?" said the Fruit Shoot.

~~~~~~~

By 3:30pm, whatever warmth had been in the day had wilted. There was no longer enough blue in the sky for a Dutchman's trousers. I was on the trail of a hot tip from Radio Suffolk listener Freddie Lay:

"Westgate Street, Long Melford, has a crinkle-crankle wall where you used to live, Lesley."

Passing over how Freddie knew of Lesley Dolphin's previous address, we swept through picturesque Melford Green to park in a lay-by opposite The Black Lion. Considerable coaxing was required to shift my passengers.

"Don't tell me," said the accredited expert in the back seat. "Another wall." He held up four fingers.

"Yep, and this one must be good," I said to my mum, "since Pevsner mentions it."

*"Near the Scutcher's Arms in **Westgate Street (#23, Long Melford)** another crinkle-crankle wall."*

Does the great architectural historian sound weary to you?

Notable enough to be listed, its vital statistics are 80m in length, 2m in height, and C18. Those curves border at least part of the garden of Falkland House, one of a pair of grand properties with its neighbour Jason

House (Jason being the name of an archipelago in the Falkland Islands). Once a single massive house, it's said that distinct properties were created when two sisters realised they were seeing the same man. The story continues that after the split, he retained a key to both houses. As fine a specimen as this was, we were all fatigued: we'd hit a wall. I dug deep.

"Hold up those fingers again." Nephew obliged. "Final finger," I announced, and drove us through the very long bit of Long Melford: gallery, tearoom, salon, antiques, repeat. "Eyes peeled for a church."

On the same side as the Co-op is a lovely symmetrical house called The Manse. Next to that, mostly hidden by a towering tree, is the library. Into the adjacent lane we trudged. Skittering hither and thither like a toddler's crayon was a half-height serpentine that protected the garden of the **United Reformed Church (#24, Long Melford)**. Historic England hedges its bets: the wall is either C18 or C19. Like Westgate Street, it also merits observation by Pevsner:

"Churchyard has one of the welcome undulating or crinkle-crankle walls."

It had been an awfully long day. This fifth wall was fine. Then I climbed a buttress to obtain a better view and saw it for the weaving wonder that it is. How tall is it? Danny De Vito would tower over it.

Sensing the end, grandmother (blue fleece) and grandson (red jacket) grimaced for a quick photo. We sought coffee and cake in the neighbouring Fanny Anne's, a disquieting blend of art deco and Elvis.

"Teatime treats for everyone. You've all done very well!"

Final score: Sudbury 3-4 Long Melford, a narrow away win.

Chapter 13

Somehow I find myself married to a woman of principles. On the Monday after that weekend of five-walls-in-a-day, one of these principles kicked in: my wife does not work on her birthday. Perhaps nobody should? Discuss. She books it off months ahead, notifies her colleagues, and all's well. In recent years I've also taken a day's leave, and off we scoot for a pleasant lunch. Used to be that we had to get back for the school run but, fortunately, children grow up.

Our relationship has evolved such that I choose the venue, make a reservation and then tell her when we need to leave. It's midday: roll up for the magical mystery tour! No doubt this control freakery goes back to some childhood trauma.

We drove north on the A14 past the A140 turn-off – "Not Bungay again, I see" – kept going past Woolpit – "Shame, I was looking forward to The Leaping Hare" – and had our pick of spots on the face of an un-crowded Bury St Edmunds car park.

"Ooh, a new place. You've been there before, I suppose?"

"Nope," I said, "but the reviews are promising." I had my fingers crossed.

Uncharacteristically early, and fittingly nippy for January, we strolled through the Benedictine ruins in the abbey gardens. Usually I'd be kicking a ball or throwing a Frisbee with the kids. Being free of that responsibility, if only briefly, still felt a tad alien.

The One Bull, allegedly over 600 years old and at one time "a sleazy dancing house", has reinvented itself as a gastropub. It's partly embedded in the abbey wall, I noticed, and decided not to use that "w" word aloud.

Not bad gnocchi, more-ish monkfish and an espresso that made you want to partake of some sleazy dancing: job done.

After a waddle up to the many-floored Ottakar's bookshop (sorry, Waterstones) where my wife picked up the new Elizabeth Strout – "Let me buy that: I can refuse you nothing today" – we ambled back to the motor.

"No need to rush back," I said.

"If you're sure…"

"…that The Boy will be fine? As long as he's remembered his key." That wasn't the cleverest thing to say, I realised. "I thought we'd have an afternoon cuppa elsewhere."

"Where? I don't want to be back too late."

She asks, I tell: them's the rules. "Lavenham?"

"Sounds good. It's been a while. I'll text him on the way."

The old Roman stretch of the A134 took us south by Great Whelnetham and past the fantastically named Bradfield Combust, reputedly named for when a mob – why are they always so angry? – took their torches to the king's hall. That village name goes back 700 years, predating The Old Bull.

Left on the Lavenham road and the day was proceeding without a kink. "OK if we do a very brief diversion? It's just that…"

She didn't look up from her phone. "There's a wall nearby, isn't there?"

"Yeah. I'll be quick."

Cockfield, local pronunciation uncertain, lies amidst a verdant Dulux catalogue of hamlets including Cross Green, Great Green, Colchester Green, Buttons Green, Gartside Green, Windsor Green and Lawshall Green. I may have made up one of those. Having parked by (but not on) the triangular village green – I didn't want the preservation society after me – I edged back along the verge, wot no pavement, in search of **Tudor Cottage (#25, Cockfield).**

Facing me across the surprisingly busy A1141 stood a clutch of bulbous bays as if piped there from a giant icing bag. Historic England have the cottage listed as C17 and remark that "the front is protected by a modern crinkle-crankle wall built of old bricks". That comment was how I discovered this example. About my height and in good nick, it's hard to miss though I bet many motorists do just that. Maybe this newer wall

58

replaced an older predecessor?

Photos were taken for my many social media followers before I jogged back to find the birthday girl calmly seated and scrolling.

"Funny," I said. "Today's the 25th and that's the 25th crinkle-crankle wall I've seen."

"Fascinating, darling. Can we get that tea? I'm spitting feathers here."

Like I say, a woman of principles.

Intermission – Why?

You've all been remarkably patient while I've been wittering on about walls. That's very much appreciated. We've already seen the long and the short and the tall (bless 'em all) with specimens ranging from those over 200 years old to those built since you were born. But why oh why oh why would you want to build a crinkle-crankle wall?

Let's dip into the brick-lined well of writings, for yes, there are writings.

Each time I ask Mr Google about crinkle-crankle walls, something I do on a regular basis, one of the above-the-fold results is a 2009 article by Trevor James entitled *Out And About Looking at Crinkle-Crankle Walls*. This was published in issue 101 of The Historian, a magazine from *The Historical Association*. They were founded in 1906 which makes them, as Victoria Wood said, totally bona fido.

Illustrated by that Wikipedia photo of Bramfield by Nat Bocking, James mentions a "rational and scientific explanation for the emergence of this form of walling". I trust you're now on the edge of your sofa.

He explains how "this type of wall trapped the sun's rays" and thus aided "the growing of fruits, especially rarer types such as peaches and figs." That classifies it as a "brick forcing wall", which brings us back to beloved Pevsner. In the introduction to his Suffolk volume, he describes crinkle-crankle walls as "undulating forcing walls of brick". This, says James, "was the primary function of this type of wall design."

Can you feel the force?

Next is a 2005 article written by Polly Burns simply titled *Crinkle-Crankle Walls* from the newsletter of the Suffolk Gardens Trust. Attentive readers may recall the Trust as the folk who published Edward Martin's piece, *Where are all the crinkle-crankle walls?*

In 700 fact-filled words, Burns informs us that such walls "evolved from the early Hortus Conclusus", a term meaning 'enclosed garden' (and well worth further investigation); that "the earliest recorded version of this 18th century wall was shown on a 1736 plan of East Horsley, Surrey"; and that these walls provided "a sheltered environment in which more tender fruit such as peaches and apricots could be grown". Also, they were normally constructed "east-west to take advantage of the sun."

If you're moving to the country, it seems, you're going to eat a lot of peaches. After all, the village shop probably closed some years ago.

We should also heed the words of Lady O'Neill of the Maines, friend of the Mitfords and famed English horticulturalist. As plain Jean O'Neill, she wrote an article in the 1980 edition of *Garden History* entitled *Walls in Half-Circles and Serpentine Walls*. She begins unequivocally: "The object of serpentine walls was, of course, for growing fruit."

I hope you're savouring that "of course" as much as I do.

O'Neill, who I suspect knows of what she writes, leads us from Sir Hugh Platt (in 1608) talking of "Quince growing against a wall lying open to the sunne" to Sir Francis Walsingham (in 1653) describing his espaliered apricot trees ripening three weeks earlier than in his orchard.

Peaches, figs, apricots, quince: juicy fruit grown on wriggly walls. And that, dear friends, is why you'd build a crinkle-crankle wall. Or is it?

The oldest of these three articles is from 1980. In pop music terms, they're all post punk. But when the wall at Heveningham was going up in 1796, Beethoven was gearing up for his first symphony. I feel we should check in with someone from that era.

The term 'arboretum', meaning a garden of trees for scientific study, was coined by the Scottish botanist John Claudius Loudon. Friend of Dickens, he produced *An Encyclopaedia Of Gardening* in 1822 where he states that "The wavy or serpentine wall has two avowed objects; first, the saving of bricks... the next proposed advantage is shelter from all the winds."

Ah, the saving of bricks. Time to retrace our steps.

Halfway through her article, O'Neill writes that "despite the fact that crinkle crankle walls were in reality longer than a straight wall, being only half the thickness, there was a saving of one third in bricks."

Burns concurs: "The walls are usually of a single brick construction... whereas a straight wall of the same length and height would have to be double skin and buttressed."

So, the soft fruit, yes, but also fewer bricks. Got it. Two reasons.

Hold on, though, because Polly Burns adds that they may have developed "because the serpentine curve became fashionable in gardens." Hogarth merits a mention here, as does the Serpentine in Hyde Park, plus Capability Brown who planned the gardens at Heveningham. There's that name again.

But Burns also feels obliged to bring in another factor, an odd one, that being the relatively minor cost of paying your men in the 1790s.

In summary, then: fruit, bricks, fashion, cheap labour.

To complete our circle, let's revisit that first piece by Trevor James. In Easton, he says, it's believed that their record-breaking wall was built "so that the Duke and Duchess of Hamilton would not see the local villagers as they made their way to church."

I hope that's answered your question.

Chapter 14

Flicking through all TV channels in my youth didn't take long: BBC1, BBC2, ITV, done. On the Beeb I'd sometimes encounter the comforting face of Ipswich-born Brian Cant. He'd been on Play School forever, and though I rarely played my Play Away LP anymore, I was perfectly happy to delay my 'O' Level revision to watch his new series, *Bric-A-Brac*.

Brian played the bumbling and bespectacled owner of a junk shop – if remade now, they'd call it Brocante – who helped the nation's literacy by concentrating on one letter and its sound each week. For example, in the "G" episode while grabbing Gus from Grantham's garden gate, he wonders aloud: "Where's the gubbins for gettin' the grime off the gate?" Imagine that in Brian's broad Ipswichian brogue.

Bric-A-Brac was bobbing in my brain because less than a week after our birthday bash at the One Bull, I was back in Bury St Edmunds for The Boy's badminton. Doing my best not to be the pushy parent, I left him debating a line call with his put-upon doubles partner and wandered into town for coffee and a paper. When I returned, all the tournament kids were lined up for a parental photo-op against a mint green sports hall wall. He stood two bricks taller than the rest, helped by a heavily gelled quiff. Driving home, we discussed his performance.

"No medal this time?"

"We would have done if it wasn't for stupid…"

"Yeah, yeah. You hungry?"

He didn't have to think. "Bacon. I need bacon."

"OK, we'll buy a baguette."

Once the greasy plates were rinsed and stacked, the remains of the day were mine and I knew precisely how to spend them. Earlier that week I'd received an anonymous tip-off from the birthday girl on the Multiyork.

"I was using Google's satellite view today…"

"In the pursuit of your professional duty?"

"In the pursuit of my professional duty, naturally, and I found something that might interest you."

I waved a dandyish hand.

"Brace yourself, but I've found some crinkle-crankle walls in Ipswich. Walls, plural."

~~~~~~~

Under a watery blue sky I zoomed off on my trusty rust-free Boardman bicycle: two wheels good, yes? Pedalling up Anglesea Road is always a masochistic pleasure, very welcome after my dry-cured streaky lunch. Underneath the massive monkey puzzle then left into Warrington Road, still climbing. Ante meridiem, Bury St Edmunds; post meridiem, **St Edmund's Road (#26, Ipswich, private).** I propped my pushbike against the kerb, locked the back wheel to the frame and considered my next move.

Previous serpentine sightings had been either on the public highway or visible from a driveway or footpath. By contrast, my objective here was located behind an impenetrable row of imposing houses. One of these served as the residence for the head of Ipswich School who could exit the back gate and stroll over to the fee-paying establishment where they "create extraordinary futures", which is nice.

Come on Rodney, I said to myself: he who dares, wins. I randomly picked a house two doors down from the headmaster's and pushed open a black gate – grime-free, note – and knocked on a door. You'll sound like a nutter, I thought.

"Can I help you?" He was about my age. No, younger.

"Hi. This might sound odd but I'm trying to track down all the crinkle-crankle walls in the country. Sorry, not country, county. Suffolk."

"Right…"

"And I hear you have such a wall…" – I could discern the start of something down the side – "which I was hoping I could see? Is that OK?"

I'd turned into one of those people outside Debenhams who ask if you've got five minutes for cancer research.

He barely blinked. "I don't see why not. Go through. I'll be inside if you need me."

"Cheers. Could I take a photo or two?" I waved my phone.

"Knock yourself out." With that, he retreated into the warmth.

What a nice man, I thought, opening the side gate. Don't ask, you don't get, Matthew 7:7 and all that.

As sure as eggs is eggs, the something that I'd glimpsed started straight and true before deciding to express itself through the medium of dance. I tiptoed along the paving slabs that separated the moss-topped shoulder-high serpentine from the smart lawn. An opening at the bottom of the garden gave access to a private road and Ipswich School playing field. I edged along the road to view the next garden, fully expecting to be yelled at by a mortarboarded master, and beheld another crinkle-crankle.

This panoply of posh properties with their jettied gables and Venetian windows sprung up in the 1890s and were the work of Ipswich architect Edward Fernley Bisshopp. You read that correctly: double 's', double 'p', like Mississippi. EFB, whose initials I'm delighted to share, lived on this very road at number 15 in a house of his own design. As Diocesan architect he worked on many local churches and played an unintended part in the serendipitous discovery of the Wenhaston Doom.

Articled to Bisshopp was a young man named Charles Wade who would progress to work on the Hampstead Garden Suburb and design – checks notes – the Great Wall, an edifice giving the illusion of a city wall.

That satellite view shows the long green gardens of house numbers 1, 3, 5, 7 and 9: five houses, four crinkle-crankle boundary walls. When *Bric-A-Brac* finished its initial run in November 1980, number one was *The Tide Is High* by the mighty Blondie. Which got me wondering: can neighbouring crinkle-crankle walls form parallel lines?

~~~~~~~

Twenty-four hours later found me loitering in an Eye car park. With me were my wife and my mum, all keen for fresh air following another Sunday roast. We were eyeballing Michael's Gate, a 1997 sculpture intricately crafted from two sections of oak to form a mystic portal. On one column sits an eagle, on the other a swan. Through this very structure, apparently, travels a ley line on its witchy way past the public toilets to Eye castle and its ultimate destination of Hopton, home to the World Indoor Bowls Championship. Ever noticed how those woods curve in mysterious ways?

Although we'd only just stepped out of the car, the day was somewhat dank and chilly and I fancied a warming beverage.

"The Bank's still open," I said. "Quick cuppa?"

"But it's quarter-to-four," said my wife. "We can't go in now."

"They shut at four. That's ample time."

"I'm not getting involved," said my mum.

"The place is about to shut," protested my wife.

"Not for another fifteen minutes. I'm going in. Coming?"

The three of us shared an awkward brew in the atmospheric surrounds of the former HSBC bank, its wooden panels reminiscent of Captain Mainwaring's branch at Walmington-on-Sea. Despite that ley line, I sensed a negative energy. It wasn't just the tea that was strained. Withdrawing from The Bank – it was now closing time – we gave our regards to Broad Street. Ahead was Lambseth Street and Chandos Lodge (#3). If I had a penny for every time some well-intentioned soul has asked if I've seen that crinkle-crankle wall at Eye, I could afford a Freddo. We'd ticked off that example three months previously in the first flush of this quest. Word on the street, however, was of other Eye sites. Right at the pharmacy and right again led us into **Buckshorn Lane (#27, Eye).**

"Somewhere down … here!" I said, a little too loudly for the sabbath. Immediately to our right was a barn that held up a brick lean-to, beyond which a wavy wall wriggled out of sight.

"That's it?" asked my mum, angling her head to get a better look. A silver people carrier, a stained picket fence and a dark varnished shed conspired to obscure our view. Unimpressed by our proximity, a pure white cat lay on the shed roof with its rear end nearly touching the late C18 brickwork. Car and cat most likely belonged to the white house next door, Wall Cottage. We perambulated past the library and another car park – visit Eye! – and collectively breathed in through the "Unsuitable for wide vehicles" sliver of Buckshorn Lane. Emerging on to Castle Street, we took a left. I nodded at the sizeable pile facing us over the road.

"Stanley House, I presume. Pevsner describes it as long and irregular. Over 400 years old in parts." While my mum murmured her assent, my wife's demeanour resembled that cat. Advising what can and (Brian) can't be done to such aged properties is what she does, and not how she'd choose to spend her weekend.

"I take it there's a wall?" she asked.

"Yep, round the back."

"Well, you're not going to see that, are you?"

I'd heard sounds of life from the garden. "Watch me," I said, and crossed the road to tap on the black gate. There followed a repeat of my conversation from St Edmund's Road. I was nine years old and asking for my ball back. I had a supplementary request.

"And would it be alright if my mum comes in too?"

Geoffrey, our genial host and the owner of **Stanley House (#28, Eye, private),** was most obliging, abandoning his chores to offer us a mini tour. His very own C18 wall has two distinct stretches, one taller than the other, neither massive, both built of red brick in the usual stretcher bond. He clearly had his work cut out since the higher part had visible repairs ("I removed some ivy") while the lower part had actually collapsed in places.

"Lovely wall," charmed my mum. "Why's it fallen down?"

"Tree roots," answered Geoffrey. "Chop the tree or abandon the wall?"

Historic England describe the coping bricks (those on top) as "canted" – it's that man again – meaning they're angled and provide a clean line. Geoffrey's wall is also propped up by the odd brick pier; there are times when we all need support. And where was my lovely wife during this episode? Biding her time on the opposite pavement and seemingly a tad miffed.

"Sorry. I thought I'd ask since we were here."

"You're an embarrassment," she replied, quoting a Madness single that shared the top 10 with *The Tide Is High*.

As we left the spectacles of Eye in our brake lights, the Qashqai's headlights magically turned on to illuminate that Chandos Lodge serpentine. Sunday, 5pm, dying light: home time, surely?

"One more, five minutes away?" I appealed to my fellow travellers. An answer came there none.

~~~~~~~

Brome Rectory was built in the mid-19th century. Clearly the Street View car doesn't come here often since Google still shows signs for The Cornwallis, "country hotel and restaurant". That's still its function but it reopened in 2014 as **The Oaksmere (#29, Brome).**

Parked in the swish courtyard, I was clearly on my own for this one. With nothing obvious in sight, I made my way into the hotel bar.

"Hi," I said to the barman, "could I see your crinkle-crankle wall, please?"

Poor lad couldn't help me but another young guy got up from a nearby chair. "This way," he said, leading us back out and over a muddy patch of land. "We're hoping to build an icehouse over there."

"Oh?"

"Here's your wall. If you're happy enough, I'll get back to my drink."

Screwing my eyes into the gloaming, I realised I was in an old kitchen garden of some size. The brickwork loomed over me and slithered away into the distant darkness. James Bettley, who updated the Suffolk Pevsner, tells us this was constructed by Daniel Penning in 1848. Shuffling along, I observed that one stretch had completely gone, leaving an arty diagonal line of exposed brick ends. Sad, but fascinating to view the innards of that single brick thickness.

Dimly lit photos grabbed, I compiled some placating phrases in my head and jogged back to the car.

Chapter 15

When you take half a day's leave from your paid employment to go and visit a crinkle-crankle wall, you know you're on a quest. Half-two on a Friday afternoon, the February sky not doing a great deal, and my mum and I were 15 miles north-east of Ipswich trying to find our turn-off.

Around 35 years earlier, my dad and I, together with older brother, were on that same road. Finding our turn-off would have been a cinch since everybody was going the same way – to an air show at RAF Bentwaters. Not sure if Uncle Sam's boys were still overpaid but they were still over here, grilling burgers, hawking grape soda, and showing off their F-15 Eagles and F-4 Phantoms. My favourite was the recently deployed A-10 Thunderbolt, a fixture of the East Anglian sky with its unmistakable twin turbofan and a terrifying rotary cannon embedded in its nose, hence its Tankbuster nickname. Being in my early teens, I'd bought the Airfix kit from Everybody's Hobbies in town, assembled it in my shared bedroom and painstakingly painted the surfaces with M13, light aircraft grey. Although pleased with my 1:72 version, I was itching to see a full-size one. I'd later discover that while I was salivating over military hardware, my future wife was joining CND and visiting Greenham Common. We each had our own unique means of coping in that Protect & Survive era, us Cold War kids.

The Americans moved out in 1993; well, most of them. One stayed behind and eventually married my sister.

With the defunct airfield to our left, Mum and I came in for another low-level pass of the B1069. "There!" yelled my mum, looking back over her shoulder as we flew past the black and white Rendlesham sign near Ivy Lodge, a mock Romanesque gatehouse that, like Anthony Perkins, pretends to be Norman.

"OK. Roundabout's up here. We shouldn't be too late."

My timekeeping is poor – I'm prone to setting off at the precise time I should be arriving – yet this particular appointment felt somewhat more important than, say, my usual lunch dates at work. It had come about as a result of my earlier Radio Suffolk and Twitter appeal, in response to which a local company had posted the most extraordinary picture of their wavy wall.

"Could I come for a quick visit sometime pls?" I gushed.

"Of course. We would love to show you around. Call us!" they tweeted back.

Blink and you'll miss a modest sign featuring a teensy arrow and one word, Stokes. "In we go," I said. My mum reached for her comb. Through some trees, along a fair length of track and finally to the unassuming headquarters of Stokes Sauces, whose aim is "to produce the best sauces you can buy in a jar".

For years The Boy was a fussy eater. Greens? No. Beans? No. Go out to a caff and present him with a plate of sausage and chips, though, and he'd be happy as Larry assuming that the table sported a red Heinz bottle. Unless, we discovered in some classier establishment (probably near Woodbridge), they offered the Stokes variety, in which case he'd be grinning like Gielgud.

Meanwhile, at Ketchup Central, the owner was striding towards us, hand outstretched. "Hi," he beamed, "I'm Rick." Of all the condiment joints in all the villages in all of Suffolk, we'd walked into his. "You must be Ed?"

"I am. Thanks so much for doing this. And this is my mum."

"Hello," she said. "I'm Margaret." Which tickled me since my wife of many years has never been given permission to use that form of address.

"Lovely. And you're here to see my wall, is that right?"

Off we strolled, Rick finishing a mug of tea and leading in his puffer jacket, blue jeans and scruffy trainers; not your typical managing director.

Rendlesham Hall (#30, private), the grounds of which we were touring, dates from the turn of the 18th century. The original burned to the ground in 1830 and was rebuilt 40 years later only to suffer the same fiery fate around 1898. Over Rick's shoulder towered a fantastic Gothic archway, an isolated remnant of the first structure. When the Women's Land Army moved out after WWII, the Sheepshanks family acquired the estate. By that time there was no hall; it had been demolished in 1949. Rick and family live in the old head gardener's house.

"Back in the day," said Rick, "there'd be over 30 gardeners working full time here" – we were staring at a giant 4m tall (straight) brick wall – "and they'd be growing grapes, cherries, nectarines and all manner of soft fruit. Most of it would be carted to Woodbridge and put on the train to London."

Something was moving beyond the wall. "Those are my rheas," explained Rick. "I'm fond of rescue animals. Over there are my peacocks and these are my Brahman Indian cattle." Holy cow!

On we walked, Rick telling us tales of walking his prize pig through the woods and about some of his random jobs (sheep farming, lumberjack) in far-flung parts of the world. We were now cutting through the vast walled garden. "Massive greenhouses were lined up over there. Figs, melons. Also used for forcing strawberries." To do what?

Through an opening, then our host inclined his head towards the middle distance. There was the sizeable crinkle-crankle wall. In decent nick and around 30 bricks tall, it runs at an odd angle to the northernmost side of the enclosed area. Were there delicately espaliered fruit trees in the many concave sections? No, there were wallabies. Actual, live, furry wallabies.

"Are we safe here?" asked my mum. I think we were both imagining being trampled underfoot or remembering old cartoons of boxing kangaroos.

"You'll be fine," reassured Rick. "They keep the grass in order for me."

As we edged nearer the well-weathered wall, cameras poised, the small gang of Australian macropods bounced off, an extraordinary sight. I suspect that the wall's intended use for growing fruit had been superseded by the rise of affordable glass, hence the greenhouses.

Where do you go from there? Well, in addition to being a regular Dr Doolittle, Rick is a committed dendrophile: the man loves trees. Larches and limes, cedars and redwoods, all have a place in his grounds and command his respect. My mum dropped back to take a telling picture of

71

Rick and I admiring a magnificent multi-trunked example: I'm idly chatting while Rick is staring heavenwards into the branches.

Taking a different pathway back, we passed the orangery that he employs as his personal Buddhist temple. "Do you know what you should do if you meet the Buddha?" I asked. Rick shook his head. "Well, they say you should kill him," I said. "It's a riddle." That gave us food for thought for the next few minutes. He invited us to view the icehouse, comprising thousands more bricks, then we were back by the car.

"Oh," said my mum, "I meant to tell you how much I like your ketchup. As does my grandson!" Honestly, that mother of mine. The sauce!

"Wait there," said Rick. He nipped into an outbuilding and returned with a four-bottle multipack of Stokes Real Tomato Ketchup. "All yours, Margaret," he said, "with my compliments. Thanks for coming. Keep well."

~~~~~~~

"Wow," said my mum, clutching her freebies in the passenger seat.

"Indeed," I agreed. "He's like that chap in the old AA advert. A nice man. A very nice man."

"What now: tea and cake?"

"Well, it so happens we have a second appointment this afternoon. Should take us about twenty minutes to get there."

"We do? And then tea and cake?"

"Definitely."

~~~~~~~

Pal Andy, fellow ping-pong player and founder of our long-lasting light lunch endeavour, kindly keeps his ear to the ground on my behalf. Incidentally, in lieu of our usual Friday outing we'd had a café trip the previous day to Smokey Joe's in downtown Ipswich. You'll be fascinated to learn that I had the Big Tuna, a grilled tuna steak with mint chilli sauce. Andy, who struggled to finish his New Yorker, double chicken plus double cheese, had told me a fortnight earlier that he'd (unbelievably) unearthed a bendy wall in his own tiny village in the back-of-beyond. I'd swapped emails with the owner; we were due there about now.

A little after 4pm, the light clinging on, we coasted along the metropolitan main street of Boyton: population in 2011, 147. No shop, no pub. At various times the village has been home to ancient hunters, smugglers, and a tank range. Recently it's become a destination for twitchers due to the chunk of nearby RSPB-owned land.

More or less opposite Andy's country house, we pulled into the gravel drive of **Clock House (#31, Boyton, private).** The owner, Richard – not Rick -- appeared as if by magic while we were still alighting from the Qashqai.

"Afternoon," he said. "Andy tells me you're partial to these weird walls."

"That's very true. And I see yours right here."

Clock House is one of two or three properties sitting in a grassy green rectangle within a far bigger brown rectangle, namely a field. Picture a squashed pea balanced on a Bourbon biscuit. Facing us was a moderately tall serpentine that weaved away from the road to the rear hedge. Richard was keen to credit the previous owner, one Kristen Busch-Hansen, who decided to construct his own wall in the late 1990s, thus making it a contemporary of Ashbocking (#10).

Using an S-shaped template, KBH not only managed to make the snake but also to climb the slight slope. "See these terracotta tiles that he put in at odd places?" asked Richard.

We ducked closer to take a look at the patterned pieces, some of which were now camouflaged by dark green moss. The entire length of the wall had to run a gauntlet through a developing jungle, sometimes struggling to be seen. I ran my fingertips along the 25-year-old bricks and we took our mandatory snaps. "Thanks again, Richard," I said, aware of the falling temperature. "If you see any more, drop me a line."

To me it felt that we'd seen today's walls in the wrong order. Ideally we'd have progressed from the diddy one at Boyton to its big brother at

Rendlesham. No matter: we'd had quite the trip out and managed to knock a pair of not publicly accessible examples from the to-do list.

I reversed out, we waved our goodbyes, and we managed to reach the Wild Strawberry at Woodbridge before it closed. Mum supped her tea, I stirred the hot milk into my Americano, and we gazed out into the darkness, thinking of Rick's place.

Chapter 16

National Trust and English Heritage membership stickers have adorned the family motor vehicle for so long that a scrap of Cornish coast and a chunk of Stonehenge sarsen must surely belong to me. Thus the kids have been conditioned to treat piles of crumbling stonework – exhibit A, Leiston Abbey – as a perfectly normal trip out. Bet they had some interesting conversations with their mates when asked what they'd done that weekend: "We spent an hour in the drizzle tromping around some monastic ruins. You?"

Two (free for members) firm family favourite destinations, both fortified, have always been Orford Castle with its creepy passages and great views of the unsettling Ness, and Framlingham Castle with its vertiginous wall walk and great views of the Mere over to the college where, as we used to inform Eldest, Charlie from Busted went to school. English Heritage sometimes entice the punters to the latter castle with the odd historical re-enactment. At one of these, under a sticky sun, we licked ice creams – guess the brand – while a big guy demonstrated the sheer weight of medieval armour.

"Here," he said, lifting a sword, "we fight like gentlemen. After all, we're not in Ipswich."

Our light lunch trio of me, Andy and Kev had also spread our chicken wings to tick off the half-dozen or so eateries in Framlingham, from the does-the-job jacket spuds at the Bridge St Café to the delicate tartlets at Kitty's. Getting there and back in one hour from Martlesham meant bending the space time continuum: let nobody doubt our dedication.

Thinking I knew the place, then, it came as a mild surprise to see Framlingham in Edward Martin's list of wavy wall sites, reportedly at somewhere called Greystones. That was reinforced by Patricia Bridges, a

Lesley Dolphin listener, who pinpointed "one behind a bungalow along Mount Pleasant". Which would explain why I could see diddly-squat on Street View.

As with Sudbury I sought hyperlocal help via Twitter, this time in the form of an aspiring novelist named John Brassey. Never met him but his blog told me that he enjoyed metal detecting, that he and his wife had won Channel 4's *Treasure Hunt* in 1988, and that he'd retired to Fram. I imagined John as a sleeper agent; that made me the Smiley of serpentines. Now activated, his training kicked in.

> [John] *You can see that there is a wall but you can't see if it is a crinkle-crankle wall.*
> [me] *OK. That's unfortunate. Thanks for checking it out.*
> [John] *If you are not in a hurry I can knock on the door and ask.*
> [me] *Please do!*

I'd have been happy to pick up a roll of microfilm from a dead drop outside the Dancing Goat, but, star that he is, he sent me some unencrypted photos. Pleased as I was to receive these snaps, the rules of this quest, which I'm merrily improvising, dictate seeing the wall in person.

~~~~~~~

Within 48 hours of our outing to Rick's Rendlesham menagerie, me and my mum (obviously) were at the fringes of Fram accompanied by (less obviously) The Boy. This was a new crew permutation. Previously he'd only have tagged along if there was ping-pong in the offing. I'd jokingly suggested that he join us that lunchtime:

"I'm in," he said.

Was he between girlfriends? I didn't like to ask.

At the Clarke & Simpson (Charlie from Busted's dad) roundabout, we took a left away from the castle towards Charlie's college, then another left to park by a grass verge on Mount Pleasant. This part of town was unFramiliar. I got out. My mum got out. The Boy did not.

"Coming?"

"You're fine," he replied, already mid-scroll.

Wouldn't you think that a fifteen-year-old boy would love to see his first crinkle-crankle wall? P'raps not. I buttoned up my jacket and marched off up the slight incline, my mum a few yards behind.

"Couldn't you have parked a bit closer?"

"Maybe, but I'm not entirely sure where this thing is."

Buttons Corner, said the sign. Crossing the road into a driveway between two hedges took us into an irregularly shaped cul-de-sac of modern houses.

"You sure about this? Looks like a dead end."

I remembered agent John's instructions: you have to knock on the bungalow door.

"Let me try this place."

As the door opened I felt a vibration in my pocket. I'd deal with that later.

"Hello. Am I right in thinking you have a crinkle-crankle wall…?"

"I do," said the middle-aged chap before me. "Curious. I had someone here recently asking the same question."

I was about to introduce my mum when I saw her striding away. "He's stuck in the car and the alarm's going off," she shouted.

Hardly Sophie's Choice, but what does a responsible parent do in that situation? "Ok. I'll be with you in a jiff once I've seen this wall." I selfishly slid myself into the bungalow. Concealed in the garden of **Greystones (#32, Framlingham, private)** was an antique wavy wall with trailing wisteria. A good 2m tall, it sported uplighters at regular intervals and wandered off into a far corner.

"This wall's shared between two or three houses," explained Mr. Greystone. "Part of an old walled garden, maybe?"

An 1884 map of Suffolk shows, bookended between the giant A and M letters of the town's name, a windmill (with the word "corn" in brackets) on this site, possibly in the grounds of the wonderfully named Engine House.

Zooming in reveals a four-sided area with a blandly linear northern border but a pleasingly snakelike southern border. That makes this masonic relic older than DH Lawrence.

My phone re-pinged. "Wonderful wall," I said, "but I need to go. Cheers."

Jogging back to the car, I checked my screen: three missed calls. Oops. My mum stood by the verge. She did not look pleased.

"Why aren't you inside?" I asked.

"Because you have the key."

I patted my other pocket. Double oops. I pinged the remote. "So sorry," I said to everyone present. "What happened?"

"You must have locked it when you were walking away," said The Boy, "which was fine until I leaned over to get the mints, then the alarm started. I tried to ring you; you didn't answer but Nana did. By the time she got back it had stopped, then she tried to open the door and it started again. Can we get something to eat, please?"

"Nice wall?" asked my mum. There was a definite tone in that remark.

All was mostly forgiven once we three claimed a cosy corner of the comfy Common Room caff on Bridge Street where the in-house record player was treating us to a dub version of Dark Side of the Moon. I devoured 45 degrees of Victoria sponge, my mum toyed with some chocolate tiffin, and The Boy fed his growing pains with a bacon bap. No Stokes, note, but Heinz sufficed. My mum, bless her, did her best to appear interested in my photos of another wall she hadn't seen.

~~~~~~~

Through the magic of Suffolk Libraries I'd managed to borrow the new *Buildings of England "Suffolk"* books, comprehensively updated by architectural historian Dr James Bettley. Pevsner's original single volume ran to 550 pages. Dr Bettley's revisions have induced literary mitosis: one book has become two. *Suffolk East,* from Akenham to Yoxford (612pp), and *Suffolk West*, from Acton to Yaxley (576pp). Leafing through was joyous: what I really wanted, though, was to find all and any instances of "serpentine" or "crinkle-crankle". This being the modern age, I Googled the good doctor and dropped him a line.

I was delighted that he replied, full stop, and pleased to see that he'd included two lists: one of around 30 assorted Suffolk walls by one Richard Webber and another of all the crinkly citations in his shiny new publications. Incorporating these placed further strain on the elasticated waist of my bulging to-do list. He also remarked that "Norman Scarfe, in his Shell Guide, said that he had listed 58 walls in Suffolk – it would be nice to have that list!" Too right, I said to the cat.

~~~~~~~

Dr Bettley's email had arrived on a Saturday; the next day, following our usual father-and-son badminton antics, we headed out, "we" being me and my wife of 25 years. After all, this was Valentine's Day.

"Darling," I said as we turned off the A12, "I know we're en route to lunch but would you mind awfully if we briefly dropped anchor to gawp at a wall?" I heard the smallest of sighs. Maybe she recalled her birthday trip to The One Bull. All of this has happened before. All of this will happen again.

Before children, one of my distant colleagues was a guy called Mark Wickham. An older bloke in the company used to jokingly refer to him as Wickham Market. Well, it tickled me.

Pevsner dismisses the various fine buildings here as "small fry" whereas Dr Bettley describes Wickham Market as "unspoilt" and notes that the centre of this large village is "more triangular than square". To the NE corner is sited the monument to meat that is EW Revett the butcher. Opposite is the splendidly symmetrical Grade II listed Hill House. Late Georgian, its semi-circular front wall leads into Dallinghoo Road and morphs into a 3m towering wall of gault (clay and sand) brick.

I ran my fingers over its abrasive surface as we followed its straight path, its height precluding any view of the property's rear. That wall drops a metre before turning sharply right into a private driveway and transforming once more, this time into the bulbous crinkle-crankle wall of **Hill House (#33, Wickham Market)**. Its top starts wide, protrudes, then protrudes still further to sit on a gault base. Sizeable brick posts in its centre hold a wooden gate that definitely leads to a secret garden. Of uncertain date, it's probably contemporary with the C19 house: I'd wager that many Wick-hamites are unaware of its existence.

"That's a good one," said my wife, "but can we go to lunch now?"

~~~~~~~

After lunch – let's return to that – I had the audacity to request one more diversion and we duly turned off to Parham, population 250. I knew the village name from seeing signs to the nearby airfield museum. I was searching for any pointers to Garden View, "a lovely first floor apartment situated within Parham Hall". According to suffolkcottageholidays.com it's a perfect couple's retreat – shame I hadn't had the forethought to book it – and features "a serpentine walled kitchen garden".

Parked on nearby Hall Road, I left my wife in the car – with the keys – and executed a quick recce while trying to keep to the public highway. CCTV warnings, chickens on guard duty, and a sign saying Danger: Bees. Oh, and the wall of **Parham Hall (#34)**.

The hall itself is no more; it was demolished 50 years ago. Adam and Sue Paul, the current owners, live in a smaller property. Not only is Adam a fine violin maker – his studio stood to my left – but he's a former lecturer in heritage gardening. He knows his onions. A 2014 *Country Living* article mentions the wavy walls and how they're "clothed with espaliered plum, cherry, apricot and fig trees". Much like Rendlesham Hall in its pomp.

From the farm forecourt I had a limited view. Those walls, plural, must look fantastic from within, I thought, and made a note to myself to return with an invitation.

Lunch two hours earlier had been back at the reliably relaxing Common Room with a Scott Walker vinyl soundtrack. Sandwiched between trips to

Framlingham, Wickham and Parham, we'd continued to ham it up. Gammon for her, eggy bread for me, complete with serpentine strips of bacon. Funny how, in a certain light, everything looks streaky.

Chapter 17

Wander along enough wavy walls and you may just find yourself back where you started. In August 2015 I'd visited Easton to view the oh-so-Suffolk serpentine in search of inspiration for a short story competition run by *Suffolk* magazine. Six months and over thirty walls later Lesley Dolphin from Radio Suffolk was asking me for photos of crinkle-crankles to include in her monthly column for that same publication. The circle of life is an endless round.

While waiting for that new edition to appear in the shops – well, my mum was certainly scanning the shelves in Morrison's – I scrolled through my to-do list. Rather than spend Sunday afternoon at home like Tony Hancock – "I might just as well be in bed, there's nothing else to do" – I scribbled some postcodes on a piece of paper folded to A7 and drove two passengers north.

"I love that view, even on a murky day," said my mum as we rounded the Blythburgh bend overlooking the water.

"It's a good 'un," agreed my wife. "Don't look, driver."

Within minutes we'd pulled over by the parish church of St Peter and St Paul. "Welcome to…"

"Wangford!" said my wife, completing my sentence with relish. Thirty years earlier I'd have been at my desk in the Duryard halls of residence (like Parham Hall, now demolished) at the university of Exeter getting to grips with reverse Polish notation and glancing up at my postcard of Hank Wangford, the country & western doctor who I'd just seen in concert.

We followed a lane behind the church leading to the old vicarage to view **Parsons Meadow (#35, Wangford),** a property recently on the market for a cool half-million. Rightmove had described a "lawned area of garden, partially enclosed by a crinkle-crankle wall", and I'd seen a photo on the Geograph website posted by Christine Matthews. About my height and perhaps no older than Eldest, the muddy-red bends were a tad regular for my liking. Nonetheless, tick it off.

"Is that it?" said my mum.

"'fraid so. But there's another one close by and you'll be thrilled to hear that we can reach it on foot. Company, march."

I'd had a midweek email from one Adam Little – I pictured a giant – who, despite exile to West London, said he'd recently read an interesting article in *Suffolk* magazine. He wanted to alert me to a wall in Wangford "in the garden of the house where I was born, Ivy House… The wall runs from Church Street across the garden (used to divide the lawn from the kitchen garden) back to the old coach house. Once, when a particularly heavy lorry went down Church Street, the vibration caused a minor collapse but it was all reinstated."

By the time I'd relayed that information we were facing elegant **Ivy House (#36, Wangford)**, ex-boarding school and a "two storey, double-fronted double pile red brick house" according to the Character Appraisal document prepared by Waveney District Council. The symmetry put me in mind of the old BBC *Play School logo*. To the left was a hedge, and somewhere behind that was a six-foot serpentine, significant enough to warrant a wiggly line on an 1883 map. We could just about glimpse it; I took some frustrated snaps over the greenery. Hats off to Adam for getting in touch and for having early access to the printed magazine.

~~~~~~~

Should you see B1126 in lights, you've either got a problem with the airbag sensor in your Honda or you're cruising along the minor road from Wangford to Reydon. We passed the church of St Margaret of Antioch – "that's me!" said my mum – and signalled right into a compact new-build estate. Kudos to the developers for the name Copperwheat Avenue, but must try harder with the two side roads, Barn Close and Farmland Close. Word of a wall on **Wangford Road (#37)** had arrived from two independent sources (in another life I could have been a reporter for the Washington Post). One was Juliet Blaxland, qualified rural architect, the other Celia, my mum's mate who lived round these parts.

A short stroll back on to the main road's pavement put us right in front of a svelte stretch of modern curved brickwork with one concavity occupied by a streetlight, number 126, decorated with a "clean up after your dog" sticker. About 90 miles away in Fenstanton, I thought I heard Capability Brown shift in his grave. Things cheered up ever so slightly, at least for me, when I realised that there was another section, slightly grassier but otherwise just as unremarkable, on the far side of the avenue.

"It's 4 o'clock on a Sunday," said my wife back in the motor. "We're not even going to get a piece of cake today, are we?"

"What?!" added my mum.

"I have a plan," I said. "We're heading somewhere now. After one more wall. One wall more." I may not have said those last few words aloud.

~~~~~~~

South of Reydon is Halesworth Road, and south of that, between two concrete ball topped brick pillars, is **Lakeside Park Drive (#38, Reydon)**. If you're picturing the identically named road by Lake St Clair outside Detroit, this isn't it. One of us got out to examine yet another contemporary crinkle-crankle. Succinct and sporting a stitched red brickwork skirt, the component bricks are multicoloured, reminiscent of those sweet pebbles you used to find in a seaside sweet shop. Eat too many and you'd feel a bit iffy, echoing my sentiments about this structure.

Four walls bagged, and only Ivy House worth writing home about. The good news? The Boardwalk café on Southwold Pier was still open. The bad? Their pushbutton coffee was underpowered and overpriced.

~~~~~~~

Later that week I arrived back from work to find the latest *Suffolk* magazine and a bag of Rocky Mountain marshmallows in the porch. Thanks, Mum. I'd finally got into the glossy pages of their March 2016 edition along with my snaps of Long Melford's United Reformed Church (#24) and Rendlesham Hall (#30), partly obscured by wallabies. Cunningly, the other side of the page featured an ad for the Crockery Barn (#10), saying "Don't miss the crinkle-crankle wall when you visit Ashbocking". As requested, Lesley Dolphin had given credit to the usual suspects – Pevsner, Scarfe, and Edward Martin – and had mentioned the Crinkle-Crankle Crew. Made it, ma, top of the world!

Intermission – What?

Attempting to surreptitiously slip out of the office one sunny afternoon, George, my goateed colleague, called out, "I see you. Are you off to see one of your walls?"

"That's the idea."

"What are they called again?"

"Crinkle-crankle."

"Crin-kle-cran-kle," he said, toying with the syllables. "What sort of a made-up word is that?"

"Well, George," I should have answered, "that made-up word goes back to the 16th century, actually." John Florio was a master of words who, along with the likes of Francis Bacon and Christopher Marlowe, may or may not have written the plays attributed to Shakespeare. Born in that London in 1553, his Protestant father took the family to mainland Europe when Mary Tudor took the throne. Returning to Merrie England in his 20s, Florio studied at Oxford and, in 1598, published a massive Italian/English dictionary. Within *A Worlde of Wordes,* Florio translates the Italian "seno" as "a bosome, a lap, the turning or hollownes of a water-banke, a creeke, a nooke, an angle, a haven, a gulfe," etc. Several lines later he continues the long list with "a crinkle crankle of any thing." I find it helpful to consider "seno" in the sense of a sine wave.

As Florio's dictionary was hitting the shelves, the poet Michael Drayton was beginning work on an epic poem to celebrate the topography of England and Wales, county by county. Containing nearly 15,000 lines of verse, *Poly-Olbion* emerged in 1612. In one section Drayton describes the twisty turning of the river Wye with its "crankling nookes", probably deriving the term from "crank" referring to the evasive path of a hare.

When I first heard the term "crinkle-crankle wall" I had a similar reaction to George with the beard. Isn't the phrase a little childlike, even babyish? Making our first attempts at speech, of course, we don't move straight on to "mother" and "grandmother" but rather "mama" and "nana", repeating a simple sound. This, linguistically, is called reduplication, and extends to other forms from simple rhymes, e.g. "my super-duper walkie-talkie", to even encompass a Yiddish variant – e.g. "this place is fancy-schmancy".

Florio's "crinkle-crankle" is an example of ablaut reduplication, that Germanic prefix having been coined by Jacob Grimm, one of the fairy tale brothers. Everything remains the same apart from a single vowel, e.g. "you meet some riffraff playing ping-pong", or consider the cheap ornaments sold in Brian Cant's shop. The pattern is nearly always an "i" modified to an "a" or "o". When did you last taste a Tic Tac or have a break with a Kit Kat?

There are even a few examples of triple ablaut reduplication, typically of the form i/a/o. Consider the bells in Frere Jacques or the US name for noughts & crosses.

One hundred years after Florio's dictionary the term "crinkle-crankle" had come to denote an overly ornate style. John Evelyn, the Restoration diarist who wasn't Pepys, employed it to denounce Gothic architecture:

"If, after he has looked awhile upon King Henry VII's chapel at Westminster, gazed on its sharp angles, jetties, narrow lights, lame statues, lace, and other cutwork and crinkle-crankle - and shall then turn his eyes upon the Banqueting House built at Whitehall by Inigo Jones..."

Forward to 1755 when Samuel Johnson – picture Robbie Coltrane – struggled for clarity in the "c" section of his own dictionary:

To CRANKLE: To run in and out; to run in flexures and windings.

To CRINKLE: To go in and out; to run in flexures.

One of Dr Johnson's pupils, David Garrick, did rather well for himself on the stage. His path to success was surely set in motion when he made his acting debut on a 1741 summer tour to Ipswich, playing a small part in a small theatre in Tankard Street. In 1891 that same building was taken over by the Salvation Army, and exactly 100 years later I was married there. Don't look for it now; it was knocked down for a car park.

Back to Garrick, who in 1766 with George Colman penned a play named *The Clandestine Marriage* which includes these lines:

MR STERLING

How d'ye like these close walks, my Lord?

LORD OGLEBY

A most excellent serpentine! It forms a perfect maze, and winds like a true-lover's knot.

MR STERLING

Ay, here's none of your straight lines here, but all taste – zig-zag, crinkum-crankum, in and out, right and left, to and again – twisting and turning like a worm, my Lord!

"Zig-zag," as we now know, is a further example of ablaut reduplication, while "crinkum-crankum" is yet another term for a serpentine wall and, unlike "crinkle-crankle", merits inclusion in Francis Grose's *Classical Dictionary of the Vulgar Tongue*. Propriety prevents me from passing on the definition.

In 1960, somewhat closer to the present day, Norman Scarfe published *Suffolk: A Shell Guide* continuing the series started by John Betjeman in the 1930s. His introduction ends with a quarter page headed "Notes on ribbon walls" where he states that "Ribbon walls, alias serpentine walls or crinkle-crankles are especially popular in Suffolk".

By contrast, a year later, Pevsner's *Buildings of England: Suffolk* cited "the delightful 'crinkle-crankle walls' of Suffolk", the author clearly feeling the need for a pair of apologetic apostrophes. Dr Bettley's 2015 revisions remove them entirely; rightly so.

Let's witness several of these terms in a charming 1959 anonymous article from *The Weekly Dispatch* entitled Day in the Country:

"There are not many damsons on the tree in the stable-yard this year. They hang neat, rounded, and purple, like grapes on a Tyrrhenian isle. Fresh, clean, and sweetly tart upon the tongue. A noble fruit, this humble little plum which somehow seems always to whisper of old farmhouse gardens or the walled gardens full of sun and butterflies and the murmur of bees, which you find about old manor houses. I know such a one in Suffolk. They built the wall of narrow red Tudor bricks 400 years ago. But it is no straight wall. Instead, it flows in waves like the undulations of a ribbon. The old name for that sort of wall is a crinkle-crankle wall. You will not see many of them anywhere. The joy of a crinkle-crankle wall is that each wave of brickwork is a little sun-warmed sanctuary for whichever tree, vine, or flower is blessed enough to live therein… And I think the best damsons I ever ate, plump, juicy, sun-kissed, came from the tree which stands, like a Victorian spinster with a mast, demurely in one corner of the crinkle-crankle."

I couldn't have put it better myself. George, I hope that's clearer.

Chapter 18

"Got distracted by this!" read an email from my mum. "Grade II listed! Not in Suffolk, of course, but sounds good."

The attached link revealed a thumbnail image of a wavy wall in Wheathampstead. Award yourself ten points if you identified this as a village north of St Albans. More clicks showed me the high street – or, to give it its proper name, High Street – at the top of which stood a smart green and gold signpost. That way for the Devil's Dyke Heritage Site and Parish Council Offices; this way for St Helen's Church and the Crinkle Crankle Wall (their capitals, note). If you've got it, flaunt it, not something we like to do hereabouts IMHO.

~~~~~~~

With our light lunch outings not happening due to the erratic availability of chauffeur Andy, and with the memory of that disappointing South-wold "coffee" from the previous weekend, I schemed a scheme to visit an unvisited well-reviewed café, just me and Mrs. Jones (not her real name). Both of us could likely drive the southern part of the A140 in our sleep thanks to the in-laws having lived for a while in Mellis, home to "the largest area of unfenced common land in England". Thanks, Wikipedia. Over their railway line and past the oddly sited Multiyork outlet brought us to the cross country A143, then a shimmy into Lion Road. You know the drill by now; before you dine, bag a serpentine.

"There! Eyes on the road!" My wife, there, illustrating why the A143 is such an accident blackspot. Contrasting with the off-white sky loomed a large wall set back from the road behind a low wooden fence. With nowhere safe to stop, we carried on.

"Let's get a better look," I said, signalling right into a public driveway and taking a visitor's parking space. Signs announced this as **St John's (#39, Palgrave),** a "medium secure" mental health hospital. Very much against the advice of my passenger, I nipped out to secure a quick photo.

Historic England's listing for Park House, as this place has come to be called, says there are lengths of crinkle-crankle wall on three sides of a huge 50x70m garden. Not only are those sections monstrously tall, at roughly 4m, but the edge visible to me slithered away for a good ten bulges.

Charles Harrison, once the squire, had the property rebuilt in the early 1800s with five bays and Doric columns, and a contemporary map displays some tell-tale wiggly lines to the east of a "saw pit". Part of the site lies in Palgrave and part in Wortham.

At this point enter Ipswich-born Richard Cobbold, author of popular novels about Margaret Catchpole (who'd worked for his family) and Freston Tower. Rector of St Mary the Virgin at Wortham from 1825 to 1877, he made extensive illustrated notes of his parishioners, eventually compiled and published as *The Biography of a Victorian Village*. In this he mentions the "beautifully situated" mansion of St John's, home of the "beloved and respected" Harrisons. He goes on to say that "St John's exhibited a lively and picturesque scene… when the Toxophilites of the elite of the neighbourhood made their appearance upon the Lawn."

Note that Cobbold's church at Wortham was reroofed by E.F. Bisshopp who designed the Ipswich houses on St Edmund's Road (#26).

I asked a passing gardener if I could step within the walls. "No," he said, "this is private property." Message received, I retreated to the Qashqai.

"Yes, I'm back. In fact, they told me to be on my way. Lunch, incidentally, is a mere five minutes away." I drove us to Katie's Kitchen, "the best café in Diss." Try the hummus.

~~~~~~~

Regarding local rivers, I picture the Alde as blue, the Deben as green, and the Orwell as red, due to the sports day teams at Whitehouse Juniors.

Completing the quartet was the yellow one, the Stour, which was chattering over stony ways and bubbling into eddying bays due west of me across **Long Melford water meadow (#40).** This was the second time I'd somewhat gingerly walked over to examine a characterful 2.5m crinkle-crankle wall that sat there flashing its curves to me and a windswept tree. The first time, I'd pulled out my trusty fruit-based device, hit the camera icon and watched the screen blank out. Wot no battery.

Thus I'd returned to the gate on Liston Lane and my waiting wife and mother, both of whom had been persuaded against the perambulation by a passing woman's advice to "mind the bull" – ha! – and borrowed my mum's Samsung. Fittingly, for Mother's Day, she gladly lent it to me.

Knowledge of this fine sinuous wall's isolated existence required a local, and "Barry at LM" was the man. I'd found his Flickr page with its "view from the meadows in Liston Lane" where, under the heading "Crinkly Crankly Wall 2", he asked "How many walls are there in Long Melford?" This was our fifth sighting in this linearly stretched location and easily the most obscure, having already accounted for Melford Hall, Cock & Bell Lane, Westgate Street and the stubby example by the United Reformed Church.

An outline of the meadow wall appears on an 1885 map near Chapel Green, site of the former St James' Chapel of which no trace remains. Later maps reveal that assorted Roman treasures were discovered here in 1837, perhaps around the time this wall went up, and that businesses included malthouses and a hair factory.

I took more photos of that irresistible old brick surface than strictly necessary then retraced my footsteps at record speed. We three then took a table at Tiffins for post-crankle refreshments. Here, they'd decided to serve their cakes on wooden boards: discuss. That aside, we went at them like a bull at a gate.

"Those photos are OK," said my mum, scrolling.

"Cheers," I said. "My eyes, your lens."

Chapter 19

Among the abundance of locations listed in Dr Bettley's email were a trio beginning with "H": Henham and Heveningham were privately owned estates and therefore out of easy reach; the third was Hollesley, which, if it arose during word association, I'd say "borstal". The correct current appellation is Young Offender Institution; there also happens to be a jail on the same site.

Incarcerated there in his teens, Brendan Behan was inspired to write *Borstal Boy*. Incarcerated there in his 60s, Jeffrey Archer was inspired to write *Cat O'Nine Tales*. Spending several months there in 2014 was Coulson: not G.A. Coulson, the schoolmaster who took over Norman Scarfe's list of walls that went AWOL, but Andy Coulson, David C*meron's one-time comms director.

One Google search led me and Ma to the Bawdsey peninsula, one mile from HMP Hollesley Bay, trying hard to admire a standard issue modern wall on the corner of Rectory Road and **Mallard Way (#41, Hollesley)** where, according to Rightmove, "the grass continues along the outside of the feature crinkle-crankle wall". That weird wall by your house? It's a feature! Hardly one crinkle and scarcely one crankle, but I guess they all count. Rick Sheepshanks would have enjoyed the palm tree, the fronds tickling the dark coping bricks.

Obviously, that wasn't the example intended by the good doctor. Back in the Qashqai for the shortest of drives to **Glebe House (#42, Hollesley, private)**, a former rectory and now, like the Red House (#15) at Sudbury, a care home. This was designed by one Samuel Sanders Teulon when Robert Peel was PM. Loved the Gothic, did Teulon, hence the elaborate porch in front of us and his porches at Holkham Hall and Sandringham, plus a clutch of churches.

The door was open. In we went to ask my usual question. "I'll need to ask my boss," said a young uniformed assistant. The boss, in turn, needed to consult the neighbours since they were the owners. We were hanging around in the foyer when another woman arrived from next door.

"You're more than welcome to view it," she said, walking us through, "but I'm intrigued to know how you know about it? We built it ourselves around the millennium."

I'd assumed it was Teulon's doing. Not so. Pleasingly tall, it weaves and wends and separates the owners' residence from the retirement home. Nearly 20 years of weathering has aged it such that it now blends in well with the original kitchen garden wall.

"We used to have a regular commute past Easton," explained Mrs. Glebe, "which we liked so much, we decided to build one of our own."

"Which now gets a mention in Dr Bettley's book," I pointed out.

"And if we moved," she added, "we'd build another!"

~~~~~~~

I used to think that Long Melford was really long until Eldest chose Aberystwyth to do her degree. Taking a Friday off work, we shared the lengthy coast-to-coast drive, grinning at the name "Mid Wales Wheels" and puzzling over the A44 Elvis rock – worth a Google – on the twisty last leg. Met the new boyfriend (who I'll call 2m Peter) whose shoulders were level with the top of Eldest's head, celebrated her belated birthday at the Backyard BBQ, and returned with Eldest, done in by her dissertation yet keen to catch up on the crankles.

To get her back on the serpentine saddle I proposed a late Sunday afternoon sortie to the north of the county – "It's what we do most weekends these days, me and Nana and very occasionally your mother" – and off we went, my wife up front while grandmother and granddaughter chitchatted nineteen to the dozen in the back. Despite winning mid-Suffolk "village of the year" and so holding the coveted Muntons plc trophy, Metfield (population: 400) was new to me. It sits perilously north in the curious county; above it lies a gathering of hamlets known as The Saints.

The four of us walked past St John the Baptist (Pevsner: "It is tall") and Honeymoon Row, a pair of three storey weavers' houses, to locate **The Bell House (#43, Metfield)**, handily identified by a black bell-shaped nameplate. Historic England said we'd find "a length of railings with a short stretch of red brick serpentine wall with segmental copings". A slight crinkle, a slender crankle to allow space for an impudent telegraph pole, a slim crinkle, end of. Andy Coulson served a longer stretch. Worth 45 minutes in the car? Absolutely, if you're on a quest.

"Hate to ask but are we heading back before the weather turns?" said my wife.

"Sort of," I replied. "Would that we were done."

Some seven weeks earlier we'd viewed the listed wall at Stanley House (#28) courtesy of owner Geoffrey. Later my man Geoffrey tipped me the wink about "a new crinkle-crankle on the Millfield estate on the outskirts of Eye." Another half-hour's motoring along unclassified roads passed unnoticed by the rear seat motormouths.

Opposite Hartismere School – England's first academy, note – is the entrance to **Millfield (#44, Eye)**, a new estate where they've gone crazy on the crankles. Look right, there's one; look left, there's another with a modish double brick red skirt. Heading home, we realised there's a much longer and loopier specimen back on Castleton Way facing that "outstanding coeducational secondary school".

"Good to be back," said Eldest, yawning.

Chapter 20

Exiting Pakefield to potter along the unerringly straight road that runs parallel to the coast, the spring rays warming us through the generous Qashqai sunroof, I was unprepared for the feeling of wondrousness that instantly seized hold of me in Lowestoft. Behind us was Kensington Gardens where Uncle Peewee once fell in the boating lake; to the right was Claremont Pier where I'd deposited a Met-ful of coppers in Crompton's Cake Walk; and down there on Grosvenor Road was the flat where my mum pegged our trunks to dry on the pulley washing line.

In the 1970s, we had a string of holidays East of Ipswich. Neither parent drove and the five of us couldn't all jump on the family's Honda 70, but an hour's slow train north could transport us to a promised land of golden sand. After big brother and I grew tired of daring each other to jump off the prom – he'd always win – we'd trot up to Sparrow's Nest, come back for 99s and fizzy drinks at Tide's Reach, then go to bed tired but happy. That's how I remember it, anyway.

Bridget the archivist kindly gave me a copy of a (full colour!) 1970s promotional booklet entitled *Where Broadland Meets The Sea* which is, to me, like a paddle in a warm sea. Flicking through it, I fully expected to see one of my dad's slides. Here's an excerpt:

> *"Catering as it does for the whole family, Lowestoft offers all the natural facilities so beloved by the younger visitor, and the broad, safe, sandy beaches, the wide traffic-free Esplanade, and the handiness of ice cream and lollipop provide the fundamentals for their enjoyment."*

On this gorgeous Good Friday, the crew fixed its eyes straight ahead on the slab of road pointing heavenwards. "Bascule bridge is up," my mum told Eldest and Middler. "Must be a boat passing through."

"That bridge is effectively me," I said. "About my age, a bit cranky, refuses to budge and upsets everyone."

The tarmac halves eventually descended – "Buckle up, girls, 'cos I might have to accelerate in case there's still a gap" – and we crossed, making our way into a petite "one hour's free parking" area. "Right, long journey, let's eat," I said, leading the crew through to the main drag.

"No wall first?" asked my mum. "You feeling alright?"

"Waterstones, Starbucks, Wilko," observed Middler behind her Ray-Bans. "All your faves. No wonder you love this place."

"When a man is tired of Lowestoft..." I replied. "In here."

Unpretentious "Coffee Heart" obliged with BBQ chicken wraps and BLTs plus a bottomless cup of tea for my mum. Another crossing now beckoned, this one on foot over the busy A47 that separates London Road South, where we'd eaten, from High Street to the north. Over the road, and bookended by the Triangle Butchery and the Spice Den squatted the boarded-up Royston's Curios, next to which sat a curious arched passage. An official monochrome sign on the wall above pronounced this to be the entrance to **Maltster's Score (#45, Lowestoft)**, as included on Eldest's original fridge list way back when.

The scores were and remain a set of slim and steep lanes connecting High Street, the old centre of the town, with the old beach village (known as The Grit) where the fish processing took place. Around a dozen scores survive, some with giveaway names like Herring Fishery Score and Lighthouse Score. Others didn't make it, such as Frost's Alley Score, now buried beneath the police station.

While Eldest adjusted her birthday present, a whizzy GoPro camera, to capture this score's full glory, I stopped to read the plaque ("in memory of Jack Rose, historian, raconteur and wit") on the inner wall.

"This Score leads down between distinctive 'crinkle crankle' walls. These walls have withstood winds and the passage of time even though they are only a single brick in thickness and are built without buttresses. Malster's Score [without the 't'] has abrupt turnings and in the 19th century had an evil reputation for robberies. It is said that it was constructed in this way as a trap to waylay the seamen returning to their ships."

We emerged from the dingy tunnel, navigated an abrupt right/left dogleg, and found ourselves at the top of some lengthy steps. What appeared to be a modern crinkle-crankle snaked to our right, some twenty bricks in height and adorned with sculptor Paul Amey's silver skeletal fish, a nod to previous water levels. I assume the original structure had long since vanished though I did spot an older part towards the foot of the slope. More twists and turns led to neighbouring Spurgeon Score with its own dinky wall.

There's a fabulous 1920s postcard of the view down Maltster's Score depicting children of various ages gazing up the steps towards the photographer. Sheets hang in a tiny garden, tall trees dwarf a lamp post, and, amazingly to these eyes, crinkle-crankle walls run down both sides. Hard to imagine they grew much soft fruit here, but such structures used fewer bricks than conventional walls and were a feature of both Lowestoft and Great Yarmouth, of which more another time.

Overcrowding, bombing and floods combined to turn The Grit into a slum; the whole area was slowly razed to the ground from the 1950s. Eldest and Middler were less interested in social history and far more taken with the appearance of a fluffy white cat, offsetting the brutality of industrial Whapload Road.

"Gulliver over there," I said, inclining my head towards the massive wind turbine that marks Ness Point.

"Yep," said Eldest. "Didn't we go there one Father's Day?"

"Oh yeah," chimed in Middler.

"Highly likely. One thing I know. There's no more walls east of here."

~~~~~~~

One or two cat-coloured clouds were coalescing when we pulled away from our free car park to recross the Bascule. Up again, it was experiencing one of its busier middle aged days, thus necessitating another wait. For me, this was peak Lowestoft.

"Remember that place over there?" I asked my mum. "I really, really wanted a pet rock and you wouldn't let me have one."

"No, not really," she replied.

The satnav guided us away from the South Pier along what's now the northernmost stretch of the A12. At some undetermined point we left lowly Lowestoft and entered civilised Carlton Colville, home of the East Anglian Transport Museum. I took a spot on the aptly named Church Lane in the encroaching shadow of St Peter's with its "exceptionally stately red brick tower" according to Dr Bettley.

With open fields visible beyond the car, it was most agreeable to trek by the gravestones with a smidge of sunshine on our backs and no work for a few days. Cutting through a gate, I issued instructions to the crew. "This is Rectory Road. We need the Old Rectory. Go." We fanned out either side and eliminated the anonymous modern houses, ending up by the church. When I can't find the eggs in Asda, I ask. I approached the nearest front door.

"Back there past the church gate? Ta very much!"

By the time I spun round the girls were already doubling back. "It's just past the gate," I told my mum. "We heard," she said.

Diagonally opposite said gate was a resin driveway big enough to flog used cars, and by that a path, along which wriggled what we'd come to see, the **Old Rectory (#46, Carlton Colville)**. This was our first Carlton Colville crinkle-crankle.

As Eldest filmed, Middler preened and posed, my mum examined the daffs and hyacinths in the wall's concavities as they clamoured for the last of the light, and I ran a finger along the lime mortar. A thing of beauty, and that was just the B-side. From the pavement on Rectory Road we spied a serpentine flower bed etched into the lawn while a handful of climbing plants reached for the sky.

Historic England have this example as 30m long. Late C18, they believe; pretty darn old, in other words, and worthy of mention in Pevsner's original *Buildings of England: Suffolk* as one of N. Scarfe's walls. Top notch. Almost obscured by the bushy corner hedge was a blue and white bike signpost. Lowestoft, it said, was around three miles away, but Carlton Colville felt light years from The Grit.

That evening my mum emailed some photos from a "nostalgia night" that my dad had organised back in 1992, a great excuse to show off his holiday slides on the dusty projector. One of those showed Dad's hand-painted red sign pinned to the living room door and reading *Welcome To Lowestoft And Tide's Reach*. Another showed the sumptuous spread put on that evening comprising vividly coloured plastic bottles of fizz labelled Hubbly Bubbly, burgers in baps, and a large plate of sugary ring doughnuts.

~~~~~~~

Twenty-four hours later the same crew – minus its most senior member – was active again. As was customary at Easter, we'd decamped to the in-laws at inaccurately named Onehouse near Stowmarket for a weekend of food and drink. With The Boy bonded to his Xbox, thus avoiding his GCSE revision, and my wife catching up with her mum, Dad and daughters snuck out to seek some pre-lasagne air, not walking but driving.

Within ten minutes we'd wound by the green children of Woolpit, shot over the A14 and taken two left turns to park by another church: St Peter yesterday, his brother St Andrew today. Fishermen both, I could picture them comparing catches in The Grit.

This was Tostock (pop. 500), a name that had been plaguing me awhile. Rachel Gooch had helpfully tweeted me about a wall hereabouts, and the online satellite view was stunning. Despite chats with the church warden and bar staff at the local, The Gardners, I hadn't properly established this wall's ownership.

Rachel, however, assured me it was "almost" visible from a footpath by the church; we were about to find out. Middler led the way in a smart belted raincoat – no shades needed today – and Eldest GoPro-ed from underneath a hooded jacket, stopping only to stroke the head of a friendly nearby horse.

"This way?" suggested Middler, indicating a route to our right.

Underfoot switched from grass to gravel. At the intersection of two access roads stood a post with arrows to several named properties. And over there?

"Wow," mouthed Eldest. Middler murmured assent.

George Brown of Bury St Edmunds did rather well from The Suffolk and Essex Bank he formed with his brother-in-law, and had **Tostock Place (#47, private)** built around 1812. North of the house is a spectacular 40x25m kitchen garden with, as Dr Bettley says, "red brick crinkle-crankle wall on all four sides." That's a continuous curve on all four compass points, and in apparent good nick, too. We didn't venture in though we did peer over the closed gate to admire the greenery.

The big house was later broken up, and The Coach House, now a smaller self-contained property, was featured in *Country Life* magazine:

> *"The crown jewel … is without a doubt the Grade II-listed crinkle-crankle walled garden … crisscrossed by walkways with separate miniature wildflower meadows … still as practical as the day it was built."*

Walking back to the car, Middler remarked that she'd love to throw a party in that garden. "Lights, drinks, a live band. And if you ever do get around to writing that book, Dad, that would be the ideal spot for your launch party."

We shall see, child, we shall see.

Chapter 21

Done with her dissertation on "twisting magnetic flux tubes", Eldest invited new boyfriend 2m Peter to Broom Acres for the first time. During that weekend we learnt that certain families don't start eating until everyone has their food. Key to his initiation was to participate in the new sensation then sweeping the nation: crinkle-crankling. How better to assess his suitability as a suitor than by strapping him into the car's rear seat then picking up my mum? What ensued, as the A12 blurred by, was 45 minutes of applied physics where the unstoppable force of Ma's questions met the immovable object of Peter's politeness.

Dunwich, said the sign, a placename that reaches beyond the county. Shame that we'd arrived 100 years too late to witness the tower of All Saints lose its grip on the land and join the other submerged buildings.

Dr Bettley, Martin Brown, and, most tellingly, Worzel (a Radio Suffolk listener) had all directed me to **Cliff House (#48, Dunwich)**, an 1830s private residence now surrounded by a smart holiday park of the same name. Searching for The 12 Lost Churches? That's the cute name of the resort's restaurant. I took "non-residents welcome" as a thumbs-up to use their car park. Our quintet emerged, grateful to stretch our legs of varying lengths.

"Somewhere near here?" asked my mum.

"Behind you, Nana," said Eldest.

"Oh wow," said Peter, "a wavy wall. How strange."

"Congratulations," I said, "and welcome to the club." I turned to my mum. "No badge for our newest recruit?"

"Early days," she replied.

"Harsh," added my wife.

The September 1st 1860 imprint of *The Suffolk Chronicle* carried this ad:

> *To be Let, with Possession, on the 11th of October next.*
> *A Very Superior and Commodious FAMILY RESIDENCE (known as the Cliff House) in perfect order, with every convenience for a family of the highest respectability, and late in the occupation of John Robinson, Esq., deceased.*
> *The House stands high, directly fronting the German Ocean, and within 300 yards of the same...*
> *The kitchen and flower gardens are enclosed by a high serpentine wall, including a very choice selection of wall and other fruit trees and bushes.*

Not even Peter could see over 7ft of brickwork or through a blocked opening in one of the garden's two sides. Motley patches of discolouration indicated its considerable age, as did the odd modern buttress. One of the best views to be had is from a YouTube promotional video for the holiday park. Shot by a drone, we happen to see into the garden: I spy a trampoline and a pool. Here's to you, Mr Robinson.

Wall ticked off, we reparked at the Coastguard Cottages along the road for National Trust scones and a brief tramp on the beach, listening for tolling from deep beneath the German Ocean.

~~~~~~~

I was sipping a cuppa in bed over the Easter weekend when my phone pinged with an email from a chap named Richard Farrow:

"Just to update your search for wavy walls, there was one at Brickwall Farm, Broad Road, Bacton near Stowmarket. When we lived there about 27 years ago, the wall was at the back of the farm house and not visible from the road. I do not know if it is still there?"

Later that day he emailed again:

106

"Driven past that way today. The wall is still there!"

Being contacted out of the blue with details of an unknown wall is always welcome. So, a week after Dunwich, I kept mum on the half-hour NW drive while my mum talked (mostly) approvingly about Eldest's boyfriend. A lush last leg took us through Canham's Green, Cow Green and Ford Green.

Perfectly parallel to the B1113 stood a perfectly pleasant if regrettably flat brick wall with a wooden sign reading **Brickwall Farm (#49, Bacton, private)**. Never was a place better named, though Cliff House was also a contender.

"I've no idea who owns this," I said as we pulled up. "Let's play it by ear."

"You do the talking", said my mum.

Over on the far lawn was a man seeing to his neat garden while a small child played on a swing. "Hi there!" I called, and within minutes we were admiring Mick's lengthy and aged crinkle-crankle wall, its ins-and-outs accentuated by beds of bluebells and daffs.

"I own this side," explained Mick, the perfect host, "and next door owns the other side. Shall we see if they're in?" Whereupon a helpful woman who we'll call Mrs Bacton showed us through her house and left us loons to snap away. Oddly the rear has a flint base and overlooks some sort of waterway, purpose unknown, presumably part of the original 19th century farmstead.

According to a mile post on the railway line 100m west of the farm, Brickwall Farm is 86 miles from London. Labourers would have heard the Norwich bound loco slowing as it pulled into nearby Finningham station. Naturally that was Beeching-ed in 1966. I'm indebted to Mick and Mrs Bacton for welcoming us with unquestioning arms.

~~~~~~~

My mate Martin, one of the Dunwich tipsters, tweeted me to say:

"Closing in on 50 – will it be something special?"

I relayed this to my mum as we examined a thigh-high wavy wall protecting the slimmest of front gardens outside **Juniper Cottage (#50, Redgrave)**, west of Diss.

"This titchy thing? Hardly Bramfield, is it?"

Spoiled by half a century of crinkle-crankles, we'd become serpentine snobs, but cheers to Jean Sheehan for the Redgrave info.

"Next one should be better," I said. "We have an appointment!"

A smattering of clouds dimmed the April azure by the time I'd driven ten miles west. On The Guardian website I'd found Diary of a Garden Designer, a series of articles by Tom Hoblyn, multiple medallist at the Chelsea Flower Show. In one of these he worried how leaf curl could mean less fruit from his fan-trained peach trees. "Our wall," he wrote, "is wavy, aka crinkle-crankle."

Parked at the impressive **Mansard House (#51, Bardwell, private)**, I shook Tom's hand and introduced my mum. He explained that the back of the house was badly overgrown when he first visited. "Then I tore off some ivy over there and saw the wall underneath. Made me realise this used to be a kitchen garden, and that convinced me to buy it."

As pictured online, there were Tom's skilfully tended trees scaling the 30+ bricks. Had we come in summer, we'd be looking at the peaches. Nice chat and nice of Tom to give us strangers the tour.

We celebrated seeing a crinkle-crankle wall being put to its intended use by taking the charabanc to the posh Leaping Hare at Wyken. My Americano? Delicious. My mum's face when tasting her traditional lemonade? Priceless.

~~~~~~~

Precisely 7x24 hours later, we returned to that uncharted triangle of Suffolk betwixt Bury St Edmunds (bottom left), Diss (top right) and Thetford (top left). Hereabouts was a concentration of unvisited undulations. In the course of various emails and phone calls trying to nail these serpentine suckers, Leeann from Rickinghall parish council had helpfully added another to my to-do list. C'est la vie, non?

Today's 4pm rendezvous was with David, owner of **Anglian House (#52, Botesdale, private)**, who'd been privy to my mum's landline skills. She noticed a sliver of wavy wall by the entrance. "I hope that's not it."

Then David appeared with a smile and steered us around the side of the house. To our right towered a mighty 3m straight wall showing clear evidence of repair. "Bus station the other side," he told us, "and sometimes they reverse into it. The best looking bit is through here."

Sure enough, there was a fine section of crinkle-crankle, a similar height to Eldest's boyfriend, at the end of his garden. The red tips of a hedge played against the many shades of vintage brick.

"I like your birdboxes," said my mum.

"Cheers. Think the wall used to be part of Street Farm over the way."

Dr Bettley writes that said farm was "refronted in red brick c. 1833", a probable date for the wall. Danke to David and Linda for the visit.

Chapter 22

Early May Day Bank Holiday, ten days after poor Prince's death and, abandoning our dead wheelbarrow's wheel, I texted my mum: "A wall or 3? CU@4."

First to Ringsfield, two miles SW of Beccles, where the churchyard of **All Saints (#53, Ringsfield)** – still standing, unlike its namesake at Dunwich – has a listed wall "mostly hidden behind undergrowth" according to informer Bob Kindred. Bet you Pevsner didn't hack his way through the overhanging thorns to view the propped-up gravestones. Only after extracting ourselves did we observe the far smarter side, around 60m long according to Historic England, belonging to The Barn, the neighbouring five-bedroom "beautifully converted timber frame barn".

Then five minutes north to Barsham for "a length of serpentine wall forming the eastern boundary of the rear garden" (thanks again, Historic England) of **The White House (#54, Barsham).** Alongside their tennis court runs all 45m of their classy listed example in an elegant garden with a snaking border. We could only see it from a distance but let's consider that White House down.

And finally to Bungay where Waveney District Council's *Conservation Area Character Appraisal* identified "an 18th century crinkle crankly garden wall at the rear of 54 Earsham Street." Like Sudbury's Red House (#15) and Hollesley's Glebe House (#42), **St Mary's House (#55, Bungay)** is now a care home. Their twisty and buttressed wall with its no-nonsense "Private Car Park: No Turning Please" sign is plain to see from round the corner on Outney Road and seems to sit on curved breezeblocks. They like a wavy wall in Waveney.

Snaps secured, my mum faced me. "Can we go back now?"

Pleased as I was to see the to-do list down to a dozen or so locations, I was very aware that the likes of Ringsfield and Bungay constituted low-hanging (soft) fruit. All such lists contain items that never shift. A number of mine had that scary "Hall" suffix such as the very first entry on Eldest's original list, **Henham Hall (#56, private)**. I'd been in Henham Park many times for the Latitude festival and seen neither hall nor wall. Where were they?

Seat of the Rous family since the 16th century, the hall itself was bull-dozed in the 1950s – "a few years ago" wrote Pevsner in his 1961 *Buildings of England* – since the family didn't have the requisite funds to repair the damage caused by WWII requisitioning. The wall, however, remains, and is highly visible on Google's satellite view. I dug out an email address for Hektor, the current incumbent, sent my boilerplate "on a quest / here's my website" request, and boom, I got me an invite.

George was on the phone when I made my mid-afternoon exit from the office but used his free hand to make a querying fish-in-the-sea gesture; I nodded. An hour later, me and Ma, the crinkle-crankle crew quorum, took a right off the Beccles road to cross a cattle grid. In the distance was Hektor's house. Bathing in the late afternoon sunlight, we were warmly greeted by Hektor plus wife Sarah and baby girl, all keen to indulge my obsession.

"This way to the garden," said Hektor. "I gather you've seen quite a few of these walls already?"

"I have, yes…"

"The size of it!" exclaimed my mum.

We stood in a vast grass-covered walled garden– "one of the largest in Europe" said Hektor – with a 100m long / 2m tall section of serpentine to our right. Excellent condition, too, having recently been restored.

"That's a boatload of bricks," I said.

"Replanting the interior is a job for another day," said Hektor. "You should have seen this site before we cleared it."

On one of the other more conventional walls, Hektor showed us some custom-made plaques depicting branches of his sprawling family tree. He's the eldest of eight children (with some magnificent names) and the son of Keith, the 6th Earl of Stradbroke, who was labelled "the Aussie Earl" by the tabloids.

"And over there," added Hektor, pointing to a white brick facade beyond the walls, "is all that's left of the hall."

An 1884 map locates the extant Henham Hall to the SE of the kitchen garden, then apparently split into ten rectangular beds. All that remains is a standing wall, reputedly part of the loggia, that now sits on its own among some trees, not unlike some folk I've seen around midnight during Latitude. Something about the isolation of that relic was really quite jarring.

Not wishing to keep him from his family any longer, we strolled back, said our goodbyes to The Honourable Hektor Rous, and set sail for Coffeelink at Darsham to spoil our tea.

~~~~~~~

Thursday, Henham; Saturday, my birthday. A big one, my 50th, and yes, something special was planned. At the back of my mind was an Armando Iannucci sketch about "a home for middle-aged men" where a nun tells the assembled blokes that "there is not now a single man in this room who will ever be an astronaut." Food for thought.

While my wife covered all available kitchen surfaces with tasty treats, The Boy helped me set up some marquees, then friends & family kept the doorbell busy throughout the day.

Mid-afternoon I was summoned inside to blow out the golden "50" candles on a cake made by my crafty wife. She'd scattered a handful of tiny yellow and pink iced flowers on a square green iced sponge base, then, across the diagonal, somehow constructed a reddish crinkle-crankle wall of biscuit bricks. Her finishing touch was a cocktail stick with a tiny handwritten sign reading "Private Property". Sweet.

Chapter 23

In July 1923 the Burton factory in Ipswich was hit by a fire that destroyed its sugar mill and almond processing plant. In June 1917 Theberton farm-workers watched as a burning Zeppelin – shot by an aircraft manufactured in Ipswich by Ransomes, Sims & Jefferies – plunged into a cornfield. Of the 18 crew, 15 died and were buried in the village churchyard; part of the airship's metal frame can still be seen in the porch of St Peter's.

A Rightmove rummage had routed my mum and I twenty-five miles NE of Ipswich to a tree-lined spot on Leiston Road just north of that church. Left, Wild About Birds, offering "high quality feeds at fair prices". Right, Sycamore Park, "an adult only campsite". Front and centre, **Pump Cottages (#57, Theberton)**, a row of five lemon chiffon houses, one of which was for sale, "set back from the road in an attractive courtyard behind a crinkle-crankle wall", according to the property blurb. You could drive by here every day for a month and not notice the subtle sine wave of this millennial 2m wall. Sprouting foliage acts as effective camouflage, too.

I held my phone aloft to sneak a pic over the top then knelt on the grass to snap another through some pretty perennials – blue-eyed Mary? – before we motored back along Pretty Road (an inquest into the Zeppelin crash was held by Ipswich coroner Bernard Pretty three days after the incident) where stands the Theberton village sign illustrating both church and airship.

~~~~~~~

"Sure you'll manage that on your own?" I asked my mum as she prepared to take on a not insignificant isosceles triangle of Victoria sponge.

"I'll manage. Nice place, this. *Emmerdale's* been good recently: did I say?"

The briefest of drives now found us lounged upstairs in the Red Poll Tearooms of the Emmerdale Farm Shop. "Always a warm welcome" proclaimed a sign that lacked an exclamation mark, so gaining my approval.

"There's apparently another Rightmove wall up the road in Darsham," I said, cutting off the soap talk. "How about we drop by with no warning?"

"Like the Daz doorstep challenge? Fair enough."

~~~~~~~

Half an hour later, having missed our turn heading north over the A12 level crossing for the Lowestoft line, I did a U-ey and pulled off into a driveway between two smart green and cream signs, one reading "Darsham Cottage" with "Moat Hall" underneath, the other reading "Moat Hall" above "Darsham Cottage". Fuelled by tannin and sugar, I strode up to the nearest front door.

"Hello…" I began.

"If you're looking for the B&B, it's the next one along," interrupted the woman slightly wearily.

"Actually, it's about your crinkle-crankle. Could we take a look?"

Both Mrs Darsham and her husband proved to be consummate ad hoc hosts for the next quarter of an hour, inviting a babbling stranger and his mother through their rather nice house – "This is the Georgian music room" – and round the back to ogle their (unlisted) elderly 3m serpentine. Greenery clung to those gnarled bricks and pink peonies compensated for an uninspiring sky.

A corn mill, a smithy and a Methodist chapel (marked as "primitive") can be seen on a local 1885 map. Beneath the huge first "A" of Darsham in the grounds of **Darsham Cottage (#58, private)** is a tiny squiggle that now towered over us.

"And over there are our alpacas," continued Mrs Darsham.

"Really? I must tell my eldest. She's finishing a physics degree as we speak but actually wants to be a zookeeper."

We clicked away, said our thanks, and took our leave.

116

"That went surprisingly well," said my mum, back in the Qashqai. "Two more wavy walls for my Facebook followers. Home, James!"

"Home: you kidding? According to Rightmove…"

"Yes, yes. Lead on."

Hard to think back to that pre-quest time when I hadn't heard of Bramfield since we now seemed to be passing through every other week-end. On into Halesworth where we'd ticked off the delightful Duck Lane (#9) the previous summer. About to exit the town's orbit, we turned left into **Old Station Road (#59, Halesworth)**.

"Wonder what used to be here?" said my mum.

"Anyone's guess. Eyes peeled."

It's Saturday, it's five-to-five, it's crinkle-crankle time. To the left of a wide grassy opening leading into a play area (under 14s only, no fouling, no litter, no camping) wound our third and final Rightmove find of the day. I wasn't expecting much, this being another young 'un, but it niftily emerges from the ground, rising from six bricks to gradually ascend to three times that height, as if built on a differently angled plane. Its knee-high source, like that wee wavy wall at Long Melford United Reformed Church (#24), enables the casual viewer to survey its length and appreciate the snaking coping stones. Among the best newer examples to date, agreed mother and son.

Not wishing to dampen the mood but, returning to the grisly theme of war, in January 1941 a Dornier bomber dropped its load on nearby Halesworth railway station, killing the station master, his wife and their teenage help. Their names – Holland, Holland, Clarke – are recorded on the obelisk war memorial outside St Mary's in town.

~~~~~~~

Three miles east of Theberton is the similarly diminutive village of Kelsale where, Dr Bettley told me, I'd find something of interest. More than one website cited "a spectacular crinkle-crankle wall" at **By The Crossways (#60, Kelsale, private).** An article in the *Suffolk* magazine – where else?

– named the owners as the Kendalls: Miranda, whose family had built the Edwardian house, and William, "serial entrepreneur" and the ex-CEO of Green & Black's. That's some half-decent chocolate.

As with Hektor at Henham, the Kendalls at Kelsale responded most positively to my par-for-the-course "on a quest" request and a Sunday afternoon date was agreed. William wouldn't be there, alas, but Miranda would be "delighted" to give us the tour. Such fun!

Three o'clock and we were bang on time: me, Mum, and special guest star, my wife, always up for nosing around an upmarket garden "if they know we're coming". We parked within cherrystone spitting distance of a glorious serpentine; I realised that our car was the only one there. The gravel scrunched as a Titchmarshian figure approached.

"I'm the gardener, Brian." Not Caliban, then. We shook hands, his green fingers at odds with my lilywhite digits. "Mrs Kendall's running late and sends her apologies. Can I help?"

"Shame. Did she say we're here to see your wall?"

Brian nodded over our shoulders. "There she is. If it's OK, I've got work to do. You're welcome to have a wander. Mind if I leave you to it?"

Easily taller than me and not as long as some, this fine example has become "a showcase for heat and drought-tolerant plants such as the bottle brush tree… which can use the heat of the brickwork" to quote an online article. Masses of artfully arranged greens, blues and pinks conspired to mess with my colour blindness and to hide most of the nearest side.

"Mustn't take a cutting," said my wife largely to herself. The three of us walked through an opening to observe the obverse and were surprised to discover a fancy swimming pool. "Doesn't seem quite right to poke around without the owner," continued my wife. "We should make a move."

"Quick snap," I said, "and we'll head for the hills."

That evening I emailed my thanks to Miranda and said that I hoped to see her in person – and partake of a cream tea – at their National Garden Scheme (NGS) open day later that year.

"Where now?" asked my mum from the rear seat.

"I thought we might try Wenhaston," I replied.

"Wenhaston? We're doomed!" said my mum.

"Good one," I said. "Get it?" I asked my wife, who sighed.

We retraced the previous weekend's route past Darsham Cottage (#58) and through Bramfield, inevitably, before spying the first bright yellow NGS sign. A narrow lane meandered to Wenhaston Grange, a £2m Queen Anne pile boasting stunning grounds with rose archways, beech-hedged garden rooms, and a harpist. Maybe she's always there? Very different experience to promenade around somebody's lawns when you've paid a fiver to do so.

"Everything but a wavy wall," my mum remarked to a chap who'd passed her some homemade Bakewell. Naturally he then revealed himself as the gardener, the second of the afternoon; he'd been occupied with these surroundings for the last three years, he told us, and was hoping to persuade some other clients to build their own serpentine.

"But no wall here," he confirmed. "You know about the one at Orford? They've got their open gardens thing tomorrow."

"Ooh. Thanks for that. Who's up for that?" I asked my fellow cake scoffers.

"I'll pass," said my wife.

"And that's why your crew badge has no number," said my mum. "I'm in."

Our B-road wove away from Wenhaston to wend its way through the Heveningham estate where I pulled over to allow Mum to take a photo of their elegant arched bridge in the distance.

"Another winner," she said. "That'll be in next month's Let's Talk."

"No doubt," I said. "Over there somewhere is a Capability Brown crinkle-crankle. It's been on the list since day one, and one day we might see it."

~~~~~~~

Visits to historic Orford usually involve an ascent of the castle, a walk along the quayside, and something sweet from posh Pump Street or the down-to-earth Riverside Tearoom. Years before we'd taken the ferry over

119

to the creepy Ness for a careful walk to the lighthouse, mildly freaked out by the National Trust's "Danger: Unexploded Ordnance" signposts. That was when Eldest was an only child: then a toddler, she has zero memory of that trip.

Spring Bank Holiday, twenty-four hours after Wenhaston, and the day was not a hot one. From St Bart's church we picked up that year's *Orford Open Gardens* leaflet. Last on the list of ten entries was **The Old Rectory (#61, Orford)** owned, it said, by Tim & Elizabeth Fargher. Not sure what may have occurred in previous years, but we noted that "St Bartholomew's Parochial Church Council ... cannot accept any responsibility for any accident or mishap which might occur in participation in this event."

Thankfully we located Rectory Road without incident and spotted an ivy-clad structure skirting the property on the corner. Nearer the entrance, the green stuff had less of a hold and revealed the gentle in-and-out of some apparently modern masonry. After a hurried circumnavigation of the 1930s white brick rectory – they were about to shut up shop – I asked genial Tim, painter and sculptor, about his wall.

"Well, the old straight one blew down in '87," he told us. "Eventually we got some quotes for a replacement from R&J Hogg in Coney Weston. They do a lot of churches. Have you heard of them?"

I hadn't, although Coney Weston, weirdly, was on the to-do list.

"Anyway, the least expensive of four quotes was a straight rebuild of the straight wall. But the second cheapest was a crinkle-crankle that would follow the curve of the road, and we went for that. This was about 1990. As you can see, it's still standing!" Hands up if you recall John Claudius Loudon's 1822 *An Encyclopaedia of Gardening* in which he names "two avowed objects" of "the wavy or serpentine wall", number one being "the saving of bricks". Here, two centuries later, was proof.

We strolled down to the quay for one last gaze at the shingle spit. In June 1917 a frozen compass caused a German Zeppelin to drift over Orford Ness, and it was from the Aircraft Experimental Station based there that a plane took off which would ultimately bring it down over Theberton.

Chapter 24

Eldest was done with Aberystwyth. Finals finalised, she was all smiles in her geeky *Get Your Ass To Mars* T-shirt when we met her at Pentre Jane Morgan, her accommodation. I tessellated her Snowdon of possessions into the Qashqai while mother and daughter caught up, then we sauntered to the sunny prom for an Ambassador's ice cream prior to the long cross-country return leg. Whereas Prince Charles spent ten weeks here in 1969 learning the language, Eldest, after three years, prided herself on knowing the Welsh for "microwave oven".

Two days later Ma and I undertook a simpler excursion, aiming for another uncharted part of sleepy Suffolk. Cast your mind back to Henham Hall (#56) where we met hospitable Hektor Rous, whose father, Keith, is the 6th Earl of Stradbroke. Appropriately, then, the village of Stradbroke – equidistant from Diss and Framlingham and boasting two schools, two pubs, and a Spar – has its own serpentine at **Fig Tree Cottage (#62, Stradbroke)**. This "spacious former farmhouse" has, claimed Rightmove, "a lovely crinkle-crankle brick wall" beside the driveway.

"I see it!" exclaimed my wavy wall junkie mother as we slowed down along New Street. Opposite was a handy close in which to park. Pavement on both sides of the road, a novelty on these trips, allowed for a close-up of both the central gravel path to the front door and the slinky structure to our right. Roughly chest height, and reminiscent of the front garden example at Shotley (#17), its ever-so-subtle sine wave slithered 20m or so away to the property's garage.

"I like those triangular stones on top," I said.

"And those clematis are pretty," said my mum from behind her camera. She examined the screen. "It's coming up to 4 o'clock. Won't everywhere be either closed or closing?"

"Never fear," I said, "for I have another postcode."

Half an hour's journey south-west – "Well, I've never been this way before", said my passenger – brought us to Columbine Hall, a moated medieval manor house that I'd seen was having an open day. Immaculate jettied house and setting and gardens as featured in Country Life, everything perfect under a pure blue sky, and with a barn serving chunky fruit cake. Yet, as my all-seeing mother observed, "No wall, though."

~~~~~~~

As fate would have it, I found myself in another stunning setting at the end of that week. If you were playing the *English Gardens* edition of Top Trumps and you found Columbine Hall in your hand, you'd feel confident of a win. Unless, that is, your opponent then played the card for Sissinghurst.

In a flurry of online writing contests the previous year, I'd counted myself highly fortunate to have a poem (*"Then It Hit Me"*) included in the *Schooldays* anthology published by the awesome Paper Swans small press. So when I saw they were running a competition in conjunction with the National Trust on the theme of "roses", I didn't let my total lack of floral knowledge prevent me from entering. Reader, I was over the flippin' moon to get an email saying that my rhyming words (*"A Crossply for your Croci"*) had been highly commended and would be part of their Poetry of Roses pamphlet: would I like to read at their launch event in Sissinghurst Castle Garden?

It was just gone 5pm and the general public were leaving as my wife and I approached the gate. "Are you one of the poets?" said someone in NT garb.

"Yes, I suppose so." Never had I felt such a surge of imposter syndrome.

Canapes and champagne (Fentimans rose lemonade for me) in the cottage. A meditative stroll through the verdant legacy of Vita Sackville-West. Readings from the poets (and me) at the top of the rose garden. Quite the evening, but no wall.

Leaving our Royal Tunbridge Wells B&B the next morning, my car door still held the posy presented to each participant by the Sissinghurst gardeners: creamy foxglove, green ammi majus, pink dame's rocket. Or so my well-informed wife told me.

Straight on to Bath to pick up Middler, first year behind her, then the always fun M4/M25 home. Thank goodness for South Mimms.

~~~~~~~

Barely time for father & son badminton next morning before the short hop to the in-laws for Sunday lunch.

"I've found one of those walls you like," said my mother-in-law while single-handedly preparing roast lamb for seven. "We can walk there later."

"Great!" I said, while The Boy raised a sarcastic thumb.

Mid-afternoon, stuffed like kippers, we left father-in-law to his nap while the rest of us, plus Boo the dog, set forth north. At some undetermined point we left Onehouse and crossed into tiny Harleston.

"Up here," said our leader, turning into a pavement-less cul-de-sac of dried mud. Hedge, fields and telegraph poles dominated the landscape.

"I'm not seeing too many houses…" I started to say, then saw what we'd come to see. Here on **Moorbridge Lane (#63, Harleston)** was a sweet stretch of 1.5m wavy wall, age uncertain – if I'd got my sums right, this was the 50th I'd seen that calendar year. I was snapping away when a woman shouted "Do you like our wall?"

"Very much so," I said, and she materialised through a sturdy brick gateway.

"My husband built this about five years ago," she told us. "We saw the one at Great Waldingfield (#20) then took some measurements from the one at Eye (#3). Once he got a feel for the curves, he chalked an outline on the ground and went from there. They're all reclaimed bricks, too."

"How fantastic," I said. "I met some people in Hollesley (#42) who did a similar thing when they built their own wall."

I also spied a dinky section on the other side of the house. Being out in the sticks, Street View's most recent capture of this road is from 2011 and shows the slightly ramshackle fence that used to sit here. Mrs Harleston's house is called "pulcherrima", meaning – anyone? – "most beautiful" in Latin. I'd agree. Harleston, Harleston, at last they've got you on the map.

~~~~~~~~

Credit to my mum's Google-fu for unearthing **Melton Hall (#64, private)** on the outskirts of swanky Woodbridge. However, one does not simply walk into Melton Hall; one has to seek the owner's blessing aforehand. That was surprisingly straightforward. Colin, following the noble tradition established by Rick and Hektor and Miranda, seemed keen to progress the quest. He forwarded me a self-penned illustrated history of the house which talked of:

"...a kitchen garden laid out with serpentine walls. As with many similar walls in Britain, legend has it that they were built by Napoleonic prisoners of war."

That was a new one on me. Then came his next paragraph:

"But in her *History of Kitchen Gardening* Susan Campbell queries this tradition and finds a more plausible explanation in the Brick Tax of 1784: crinkle-crankle walls could be built only one brick thick and used about a third of the material required for a straight wall of the same length."

Our beloved government had to find some way to pay for the War of American Independence. Since the tax was based on the pure number of bricks, some wily manufacturers began to use larger moulds only for the Tories to then set a limit on the dimensions. You can't win.

On the Tuesday leading up to the longest day of the year, the Qashqai tractored out of Ipswich containing more or less the entire crinkle-crankle crew. Me, my mum, Eldest and Middler, and, making a rare cameo appearance, Eldest's best mate.

"Look," I said as we passed the Martlesham park and ride, "we can't all turn up on this poor guy's doorstep. He's expecting me and one other, not the Waltons."

"But what are we meant to do while you're inside?" asked Eldest.

"I dunno. Buy yourselves a drink at the pub opposite?"

"Buy ourselves a drink?"

"OK, I'll give you a tenner."

By 7:30pm crew members 2, 3, and 4 were entering The Coach & Horses while members 1 and 5 knocked on the door of Melton Hall.

"Hi. Colin? Good to meet you. This is my mum."

"My family have been here for over 20 years," he informed us while escorting us past the half-round Doric porch and through to the blossoming kitchen garden, much of the brickwork camouflaged by well-kept greenery. Enchanting as it undoubtedly was, my senses had been affected by my Sissinghurst tour four days earlier. But Vita, as we know, had no serpentine. Melton Hall? They got a wall.

Actually, three sides of the rectangle are weirdly wavy and could well date back to the 1807 rebuilt house; an earlier building burnt down. So it goes. Scratched into these ancient bricks, intriguingly, are names such as Vermas H.N. and George Newington. If only those walls could talk.

Colin and family are clearly doing a fine job here, not only looking after the house but also managing a meadow with the Suffolk Wildlife Trust and hosting the parish fete. Photos taken, we caught a glimpse of a freshly painted croquet lawn before we said ciao to courteous Colin. Outside the pub, the kiddies occupied three sides of a square wooden table.

"Thanks for that tenner," said Eldest. "Three pints of Coke? £10.50!"

~~~~~~~

To the east of Ipswich in the (deep breath) Suffolk Coast & Heaths Area of Outstanding Natural Beauty lay a line of serpentines that we'd seen at Orford (#61), Boyton (#31) and Hollesley (#41 & #42). One that had eluded me thus far was an English Heritage-listed "walled garden to the rear of **Cedar Court" (#65, Alderton, private),** a short spit from Shingle Street.

Conversations with table tennis friend Andy, the Boyton Boy, suggested that the owner might be his old GP, recently retired. An email thread yielded the landline number of chatty Dr Ken. Could I visit next week? No, he was hoping to sail to Brighton. The following Wednesday? No, that was my wedding anniversary. OK, I said, I'll be in touch.

Finally we hit upon a 6pm Sunday slot. Mum and Middler and I, the original trio who'd visited Easton (#1) back in the day, enjoyed browsing the Lettering Arts Centre at Snape Maltings – and some flapjack at the Granary Tea Shop – before I steered us south though Butley and Hollesley.

"Wide open field to our right," I told my passengers, "then there should be a curved brick entrance to our left… Here, Cedar Court."

We three Brooms swept up the tree-lined drive like royalty and, somewhat self-consciously, parked in front of the fantastically symmetrical Queen Anne house that had eventually appeared. I half expected a butler to run out and shoo us away; instead a bloke in striped polo shirt and baggy cargo shorts emerged.

"Ed? I'm Ken. Welcome to Cedar Court. Can I get you all a cup of tea?"

Which nicely set the tone for an informal and enjoyable tour of his long and lush grounds. Ken and family have been here for thirty years dealing with sandy soil, fallen trees and the upkeep of an 18th century house. As with Colin at Melton Hall, everything's in safe hands.

"Just under an acre," he told me when I asked about the walled garden with its aged 3m crinkle-crankles to east and west, easily identifiable on Google's satellite view. "Can't put an exact date on them, I'm afraid," he said. Chatting about other examples, I happened to mention Orford rectory (#61): "Yes," he said, "I saw that taking shape."

What with the orchard and the grassland meadow, never mind the coach house and the lime tree avenue, there was almost too much to take in. We finished our teas, rather awkwardly handed back our mugs, and left Dr and Mrs Ken to a peaceful Sunday evening.

~~~~~~~

Mid-June and we were all due a break. After Alderton on the Sunday, the following Saturday found us driving the Qashqai on the wrong side of the road in French France. Our satnav was leading us to un petit village not far from Bergerac in the Dordogne. Stopping 100km south of Calais at the Aire de la Baie de Somme services for baguettes and very good vending machine coffee, I felt that the bold black & white slogan on Eldest's T-shirt reflected the Brexit result announced the previous day: Oh Crepe.

Chapter 25

June was when England crashed out of Euro 2016 to the footballing giants of Iceland. July was when the family returned to a UK where 52% wanted to take back control. May was now PM.

Life waltzed along – Eldest's graduation, The Boy's prom, Middler back to Bath – and the ticked-off tally for the warmest month of the year was precisely zero with no recount required. The walls 'n' halls on my not-yet-done list felt like ice-encrusted packages stuck to the back of the freezer. Those easily visible from road or footpath – the ready meals, if you will – had been swallowed up. Defrosting, to strain this metaphor still further, would require concentrated internetting, inquisitive emailing, and speculative phone calling to real live people.

"Do you remember," asked my mum on Facetime one Friday evening, "that I wrote to a handful of halls on the list? And somebody gave me a call weeks later?"

"Yep. What happened with that?"

"Gave me his number, I tried to make contact again, then nothing. Said to 'come any time'. He was at Coney Weston, wherever that is."

"Well, what say we swing by tomorrow? He can only say no."

"Immediately to the north-west" of **Coney Weston Hall (#66, private)**, said Historic England, were "serpentine walls surrounding a kitchen garden". Through Ixworth (not Ickworth) up to the A143, we saw a sign to Bardwell (#51) and pushed into the theoretical northern limits of Suffolk, there to enter the village logged in the Domesday Book as Cunungestuna. The Swan Inn came and went on our right and, with the houses petering out, The Street became Fen Street. Blue sky, green fields, then a jarringly white entrance to the hall. Twin brick pillars were topped with pure white bird-of-prey sculptures.

"American eagles, do you think?" asked my mum.

"Most likely, given those flags down the driveway."

Closed iron gates and a security warning may have dissuaded the casual brush salesman but not these two Brooms. My finger hovered over the black intercom button.

"'Come any time,'" reminded my mum. "He's another Colin."

I buzzed. Twenty seconds of silence. A female voice. "Hello?"

"Hi. We've dropped by hoping to see Colin's crinkle-crankle wall. He said to come any time."

"Hang on," she said, "I'm in town. I'll see if Colin's there." She was in town: how did that work? More audio nothingness. "Yes, he's fine with that. I'll buzz you through. Drive up to the house." Those heavy metal gates magically swung open.

I did as instructed. We gazed up at the Stars and Stripes. Like the one at 1600 Pennsylvania Avenue, this white house has two storeys and a pedimented centre. A small fleet of prestige automobiles formed a welcoming committee on the gravel. My Qashqai joined the showroom.

"Hello," said a softly spoken chap slipping between the motors, "I'm Colin. Sorry it's taken so long. Thanks for coming. You're here for my wall?"

Described in the East Anglian Daily Times as "a wealthy Suffolk businessman", Colin bought the house ten years previously when his racing tips enterprise took off. "I'd always lived in the village and had dreams of owning the big hall," he told us, "then it came on the market as I was selling my company." His 1,500 acre estate includes most, if not all, of the Knetishall airfield built for the USAF in 1943. B-17 Flying Fortresses belonging to the 388th Bomb Group flew from here for the remainder of WWII.

"I'm still finding fragments from when the Americans were based here."

"We saw your flags," said my mum.

"My tribute. For instance, I found an engraved ring a couple of years back. The RAF eventually managed to return it to the family in the States."

"Wow," I said. "but we don't want to keep you. Could we go and see

130

the wall, please?"

"Oh, of course. The garden's in a state what with one thing and another. It's on the list. The bees seem to have a taste for that wall, as you'll see. There are things I need to do. Are you OK on your own?"

He pointed into the distance, we shook hands, and he was gone. Off we trampled over some patchy terrain behind the house. Beyond the weeds sat half a dozen bays of authentically vintage 2m crinkle-crankle, probably dating from the 1805 remodelling and enlargement of Coney Weston Hall. Missing bricks, several nasty top-to-bottom cracks and many small circular indentations (bees?) attested to its neglect. Colin's garden, at least on the day of our visit, badly needed some TLC from Mary and Dickon. With its fully serpentine south and west walls, this setting deserves to be a thing of beauty.

After a quarter of an hour's unsupervised wandering around (but not into) the garden, we came away through the spooky gates – "Open sesame!" said my passenger – and did the short hop to Hillcrest Nurseries. There, over millionaire's shortbread, we ruminated on our Coney Weston jaunt. Cheers to courteous Colin.

~~~~~~~

Still feeling those kicks from wall #66, my mum came up trumps again. I'd sent her details of a Rightmove house in Bungay where "the rear garden is a safe enclosed space sheltered by a lovely old crinkle-crankle wall". Quick as you like she'd spoken to the agent, contacted the owner, and arranged a visit that Sunday afternoon.

"They do know we're not going to buy the place?"

"Of course. Well, I think so. We'll see."

Five of us had occupied the Qashqai to sunny France. A different five had travelled to Melton Hall (#64) though only two had seen that wall. Another set of five secured their seatbelts for this latest expedition. Myself and Eldest occupied the centre of that Venn diagram. With us were my mum, obvs, Eldest's best mate, and my wife.

"I see we're being joined by the honorary crew member," remarked my mum on being relegated to a rear seat.

The Boy had received his GCSE results that week and required Grade C Maths and English, minimum, to progress to 6th form. Thanks to extra tuition, Maths was a pass. Good boy. English, which he assured me he'd nail? Fail. Undeterred, he'd persuaded his mother to dry her eyes and drive him to Suffolk One where he'd duly sweet-talked his way onto his desired sports coaching course. He'd need to retake his English but he assured me (and them) that he'd nail it second time around.

I'd dangled the prospect of a pre-match lunch in the "long thin town" (Dr Bettley) of Bungay and had only myself to blame for the high turnout, The Boy excluded.

"Do you know it's precisely one year – 366 days – since that first trip to Easton (#1)?" I said to my captive audience as the turbines at Eye flew by.

"I suppose it must be," said my mum. "Where are we eating?"

"Here," I said, half an hour later as we walked into the courtyard of the tried and tested Earsham Street Cafe.

"This visit: just the two of us again?" asked my mum once we'd ordered.

"Erm..." I managed.

"Not fair!" said Eldest.

"What she said," added her mate.

"And what am I meant to do?" said my wife.

"OK," I said. "We'll all turn up, shall we?"

"Rent-a-crowd!" laughed my mum.

Ten to three, we left the cafe. Five to three, we blocked the pavement on Broad Street outside the pink-washed and black-timbered **Oxnead (#67, Bungay, private)**. Overhead, covering up an old business sign, hung a Fine & Country "for sale" sign. Eldest stepped forward, knocked, then stepped back into the flashmob. A woman opened the door.

"Hi," I said. "I'm so sorry but there's 1-2-3-4-5 of us" – the girls waved – "to look at your wall."

She smiled. "Come through. The more the merrier!"

Which was how we met the delightful Mrs Duckett (and eventually her husband) who happily allowed all of us to gawp at the wonkily buttressed crinkle-crankle running down the left of her well-tended garden. Pink hydrangeas and white anemones – much appreciated by my wife – enhanced the handful of boozy curves. Standing on the lawn, we had a fine view of the ancient house that takes its name from a lost settlement in N*rfolk. Less well known than the one in London is the Great Fire of Bungay that decimated the town in 1688. While Oxnead's exterior is C19, parts of the interior predate that conflagration. Historic England mention a window inscribed "1400" though maybe the carpenters downed tools at 2pm.

"My husband and I used to run an antiques business," explained Mrs Duckett, "but we don't need this huge place anymore. While you're here, would you like to see inside?"

Mind-your-head doorways, up and down stairs over three floors – a sitting room on each, the topmost with a calming view of the Waveney – and artwork everywhere. She studied the girls. "My grandchildren have stuck their names on the paintings they'd like for themselves."

Tour complete, the crew decamped to stand by the wall. "You're welcome any time," said Mrs Duckett, waving as we marched out of the back gate into Nethergate Street.

"Any longer in there and she'd have adopted you," I said to Eldest.

"Fine by me. Nana Duckett has a ring to it."

~~~~~~~

The gradient is such in Bungay that all roads lead to Earsham Street. At 4pm on the Sabbath the eponymous cafe remained open for business – kudos to them – so, ignoring Dionne Warwick's advice, we trotted back in to reclaim our table in the sunlit courtyard. Cake ensued.

"What is it you put in the flapjack?" my mum asked the waitress. "I can't quite place it."

"Loose lips sink ships," came an answer of sorts.

Finally achieving escape velocity, I suggested we take a different route back to the car; I like to give that mother of mine some exercise. "Short stroll to take in that other Bungay example?"

"Two in one day," said Eldest's Best Mate while we regarded the wavy wall on Outney Street by St Mary's House (#55). "I miss these trips."

We doubled back and followed a public footpath behind Earsham Street.

"Don't look now," I said, "but it's Black Shuck."

High on a back garden fence was a cat with a tricolour camouflage of cappuccino, Nescafe and espresso (I should cut down on the caffeine). Animal-loving Eldest, the cat whisperer, went to work. That cat just sat. On past the remains of Bungay castle - "Bigod, there's not much of that left," I said as some tumbleweed rolled past - and out by Jester's cafe, closed, of course. "Oh look," said my wife, inclining her head, "there's that modern wall again."

"What?" I spluttered. "Where?" She steered our five-a-side team towards a new-ish 6ft wall that snaked around the garden of **Castle Orchard House (#68, Bungay)**. "We haven't been here before. This is literally a new one. Good spot."

"Not two but three in a day!" said Eldest's best mate, both girls vogueing as my mum started snapping. Later Googling revealed this to be the work of Willow Builders in Ditchingham, two miles north and two steps away from the county line. They'd been employed to extend the house, landscape the grounds and build "a crinckle cranckle walled garden" according to their website. Shocking spelling. Super serpentine.

~~~~~~~~

Another Sunday, another stretch of A143. In the days of pagers when characters were at a premium, "143" was shorthand for I Love You, being the number of letters per word. I wouldn't say I loved the A143 but we had been seeing a lot of each other recently. Reduced to the far more typical mother-and-son crew hardcore, we were in pursuit of "a stretch of garden wall... arranged in a pattern of wide curves" (said Historic England) in Wattisfield. The village, Suffolk's equivalent of Stoke-on-Trent, has been associated with pottery since Roman times. Much mica clay in this neighbourhood.

"Wattisfield church" and "Village Hall" said the turn-off. "Never been this way before," said my mum, channelling Willie Nelson. We nodded at the church of St Margaret "nicely sited halfway up the gently sloping curving village street", in Dr Bettley's words, and pulled over on a narrow road, the properties set back and entirely hidden by trees.

"'Tis one of those yonder," I said. "Shall we?"

Unlike Coney Weston, we had no invitation; I'd decided to chance our collective arm on a dull September afternoon. "Fancy," said my mum, as we casually walked up the short driveway to catch our first view of **The Croft (#69, Wattisfield, private)**, a C17 pile with timbers showing. My turn to knock and repeat my customary lunatic spiel. Yet again, a complete stranger was more than happy to oblige. "Over here," said the extremely cordial Mr Croft, walking us over to that very "stretch of garden wall" that we'd missed on the short walk to the door. Ivy descended, bushes ascended, and it wasn't easy to spot those wide curves promised in the brochure. As per the listing description, the surface was curiously covered in "bands of random flint", presumably utilising freely-available local materials. A section by the corner of the house contains an arched entrance suitable for a carriage, and the other end of the wall has been demolished and so no longer reaches the road. It's a weird one. "That section now guards a shower room," said Mr Croft. "And aren't these walls supposed to have some mathematical symbolism?"

"I've seen some crinkle-crankle maths online," I said. "Complex stuff."

"There's meant to be some link between this wall and Capability Brown," he continued, "or one of his acolytes, anyway."

"Mr Brown who designed the well known one at Heveningham?"

"Of course. You must have done that one already as part of this 'quest'?"

"Not yet," I sniffed. "Not yet."

Chapter 26

We need to talk about Heveningham.

Window shopping in Woodbridge, I'd espied a promising book entitled *A Glossary of Garden History*. Author was Michael Symes, "specialist in the history of C18 English gardens". Suffolk Libraries came up trumps again and delivered a copy to Broomhill library, up the road from Broom Acres. Too posh to push, I jumped straight to the C-section.

"Crinkle-crankle wall (or crinkum-crankum). A serpentine wall, with fruit grown in the bays. An example is at Heveningham Hall, Suffolk, designed by Brown."

Nothing new there. However, Symes had singled out what struck me as the most formidable wall, in terms of access, remaining on my list. If Colin at Coney Weston Hall (Grade II) was doing alright for himself, then Jon Hunt at Heveningham Hall (Grade I) was doing very well indeed. We were doing okay ourselves, our own capability built on little more than phone calls and emails. Now, sixty-nine walls down, the completist in me was compelled to bear witness to each and every crinkle-crankle in the county. I unearthed an email address for Will, one of Mr Hunt's people, and zinged off my cookie-cutter "quest" request one Friday lunchtime. Will replied on the Monday:

"Since Heveningham Hall is a private family home we cannot arrange an individual visit, however, you are very welcome to attend next year's Country Fair when the Walled Garden will be open to the public."

Fair play. Mr Hunt opens the grounds of "the grandest Georgian mansion of Suffolk" (Pevsner) one weekend a year, a bit like Brigadoon. Posters for the event adorn many of the county's roadsides in May and June. My mum had seen several on one of our outings near Darsham.

"Look. Hev-e-ning-ham." She enjoyed struggling with those syllables

137

and liked to elongate that final 'ham'. "That's in July. Wouldn't that be a golden chance to tick off their wall?"

"Indeed it would. I'll check those dates."

Reader, I checked those dates only to discover we'd be on our hols in France. Was I irked? Yes, un peu, given the many months to wait. Back at my keyboard, I touch-typed a follow-up message to Will expressing my mild disappointment and shamelessly namechecking Rendlesham Rick and Henham Hektor as upright chaps who'd helped me out. I signed off thus:

"Never mind. I'll put next July on the calendar and keep Heveningham on the to-do list."

A response popped in next morning:

"Is there any more information you can give me on the reason for your visit? Are you writing an article or book?"

Where there's a Will, I thought, and sent him half-a-dozen exquisitely penned paragraphs summarising the last year's crinkle-crankling. Edward Martin, James Bettley and the mighty Pevsner all received their dues.

Message number three arrived within five minutes:

"I am in Suffolk tomorrow so will raise the issue again and come back to you in due course."

My mind's eye pictured eager-to-please Will (Smithers) pleading my case to corporate Jon Hunt (Mr Burns) while taking tiffin in Wyatt's Hall, "one of the most refined rooms of its date in England" (Pevsner again). I saw Mr Hunt perusing my website on a sleek Apple laptop, sometimes nodding, sometimes chuckling. "Seems like a decent sort, Will. Of course he can come, and his mother too!"

I heard nothing more.

Chapter 27

A few days after Wattisfield (#69) I took the Thursday off for a non-wall family trip to Bedfordshire. Eldest was looking for a job and then she found a job, and now she was moving in to a one-bed flat, handily placed for her new laser-based employment, with 2m Peter. What seemed to this parent like a very grown-up turn of events was slightly undermined by a storage box in the Qashqai's boot, out of which popped the head of her teddy bear.

~~~~~~~

Usually, I'm one of the last to arrive in the office. Every couple of months, however, I have a 6am start to carry out certain technical tasks before those pesky users log in. I'm no morning person but I do enjoy being there on my Al Capone, 6 Music bubbling in the background, and admiring the natural light seeping into the sterile environment. Most conducive to the maximum concentration required when tampering with a live system.

This is all very hoopla until my colleague sashays in at 8am, shoots me a 'Good morning: all done?' and, not waiting for an answer, switches on the overhead strip lights Regardless Of The Ambient Conditions. Bang go my ideal working conditions.

There's another upside to such days: arrive early, leave early. At 2:30pm on that particular Wednesday, the week after Eldest's departure, I strutted to the door and swiped out of the office. Laters, losers. In the conference room next door, perhaps on the receiving end of a quarterly 1-to-1, George gave me a quick thumbs-up. Half an hour to bike home, five minutes to change, then another ten to drive to my mum's: that 4:30pm appointment should work.

We had our longest trip yet ahead of us. With Heveningham not happening, I'd diverted my energies to the previous page of Dr Bettley's *Suffolk: East* volume which described the historic highs of the superbly named Herringfleet.

Drive an hour south from Ipswich and you're in deepest Essex; an hour north, N*rfolk; an hour north-east, however, and you'll find yourself in a sticky-out bit of Suffolk. As we knew from recent excursions to Bungay and Beccles, the River Waveney separates the northern folk from the southern folk. But on its wavy way from west to east it catches wind of Lowestoft, reassesses its watery course, and decides instead to head north for the River Yare, hence that protuberance.

"It's too hot," complained my mother, sleeveless again, when I swung by. All the windows were down.

"Yep. I had a sweaty ride back. That air's like treacle." I took a slug from my water bottle. "Should be cooler near the coast."

"Is Herringfleet near the coast?"

"Ish."

As with that modern wall in Reydon (#37), today's tip-off was courtesy of Juliet Blaxland, rural architect and author of *The Easternmost House*. Trying to identify the owner of Herringfleet Hall had led me up the (walled) garden path with insufficiently detailed web pages, bounced emails and unanswered voicemails. Then I twigged that the hall fell within the XXL Somerleyton estate. My request to visit was pinballed around that office and, when the music stopped, landed on the desk of helpful Paul, our half-four date. Rather than head directly for the hall, he suggested we meet him at the estate office itself.

Getting there involved our very good friend the A143. Keeping the thrill alive, the road ditched Suffolk near Ditchingham and wandered among picturesque Broads country – "Lovely up here," offered my mum – up to St Olaves which, until the Local Government Act of 1972 (effective 1974), was in Suffolk along with a handful of other villages. A remarkably straight B-road took us south, out of Nelson's County and back under the quest's remit. I saw a sign and pulled up behind a large barn.

Our host, Paul – good solid name, that – appeared from a back room to shake my hand. "Welcome to the Somerleyton estate. Easiest if I drive and I'll obviously drop you back here."

"Great. I'll tell my mum."

Into Paul's motor we climbed, a four-wheel-drive bearing the estate branding of an animal (a deer?) awkwardly holding a four-way cross. "The estate's quite a size," said our driver as we set off. "About 100 properties spread over 5,000 acres. You're here for the wobbly wall at Herringfleet Hall, that right?"

"That's the bunny."

"We have a lot of those up here. We'll go to the hall later, but I have a surprise for you first."

I turned my head to catch my mum's eye. What could this be? We were none the wiser as Paul stopped outside a quaint cottage. Getting out, he beckoned us to follow him into a partially wooded back garden.

"Excuse us," he said to a couple sat in easy chairs enjoying a glass of wine, "I'm from the estate. We won't disturb you for long." Unfazed, they returned to their sauvignon blanc.

He ventured into some undergrowth then stopped, turned back to us and spread his arms. "What do you think of this?"

Behind him ran a wall. An old wall. An old straight wall.

"Nice," I said, unsure of the etiquette.

"That's flat!" said my mum. Brutally honest, my family.

"Is it?" said Paul, clearly deflated. His head swung left and right. "I'm so sorry. I thought it was bendy."

His apologies continued, firstly to the holidaying couple and secondly to us, as did our repeated attempts to dismiss the matter. We were all glad to turn off Blocka Road into the tree-covered driveway of **Herringfleet Hall (#70, private)**. Once again, we traipsed after Paul, glancing to our left at the prim and proper hall with its Greek Doric porch. Past the tennis court and through a doorway, we found ourselves in another overgrown secret garden, bigger than Tostock (#47), smaller than Henham (#56). To our right and off to the left ran enormously tall (4m?) flat brick walls.

"Mind your step," advised Paul as we waded through spiky

141

straw-coloured foliage. We paused to wipe our brows and to soak up the sight of a magnificent greenhouse structure, now weather-beaten and in need of replacement glass and a paint job.

"Your wall's somewhere over there," said Paul, indicating an apparently impenetrable palisade of greenery, "but I don't think we'll be able to reach it from this side. Lots of rain, lots of sun. It's been a good growing year. Let's double-back and take a different tack."

"Hope it's worth it," said my mum, aglow in the 5pm sun.

Out and around, we cut alongside the northern wall behind the unloved greenhouse. Reddy-brown hues materialized among the vegetation. Barely able to discern a curve, I couldn't see the wall for the trees. Getting within touching distance proved fraught. My mum stayed back, snapping away.

"Sorry again," said Paul. "It's a jungle in there, literally. We're aiming to tidy the garden and chop back all of this, hopefully by the end of the year. Please tell me that this one bends."

"Yep," I said, "far as I can tell."

One Norton Nicholls, rector at nearby Lound from 1767 to 1809 and a good friend of the poet Thomas Gray, designed these gardens. The 1844 edition of *White's Gazetteer* refers to the reverend's "pleasure grounds" and "their rich variety of thorns, hollies and flowering shrubs."

We three extricated ourselves from those very thorns for a lift back to Paul's base. Behind us, the hall cast long shadows over the smart lawn.

"Hope you got what you wanted," said Paul as we parted.

"Excellent, thanks," I said. "We very much enjoyed both walls."

Herringfleet's name translates as "the creek of Herala's people" and is thus completely unrelated to those oily silver darlings. Nonetheless it seemed only right to seek refreshment in Lowestoft, once famous for its herring fleet. Our short drive through Somerleyton to the seaside inadvertently echoed part of WG Sebald's route in his book *The Rings of Saturn*, and we passed the station still sporting its vintage white-on-blue "British Railways Lowestoft Central" sign as grainily pictured in its pages. Opposite stood The Joseph Conrad, that being the name of the town's

Wetherspoon's. All the literary greats pass this way.

We parked, walked on the prom past Tide's Reach – only 90p for a cuppa – and took a table outside The Hatfield to imbibe pricier beverages and some late summer vitamin D. My mum poured some more tea.

"Do we have time to pop over to the amusements on the pier?"

"Alright," I said, "but £2 tops. That's my inheritance."

Chapter 28

Deep in the Martlesham matrix one unremarkable Wednesday morning, I sensed a disturbance and realised my phone was ringing: incoming call from an Ipswich number. Less likely these days to be somebody from The Boy's school about a fall in the playground.

"Hello?"

"Hi, this is Matt from Radio Suffolk. I think we had you on at the start of this year talking to Lesley about… walls?"

"That was me, yes."

"Well, this afternoon we're talking to a man who claims to have built the first crinkle-crankle wall in Suffolk for 100 years. Would you be free to talk?"

I looked at my actual pays-the-bills work to-do list and not my shrinking list of unvisited walls.

"Would love to, Matt, but work's a pig at present. That isn't true, by the way; there's quite a few modern walls out there," none of which came to mind. "Another time?"

"Sure," said courteous Matt. In an instant, I'd kiboshed my alternative career as a local media pundit.

~~~~~~~

Come the next weekend, the crinkle-crankle duo embarked on another Saturday afternoon spin.

"Long trousers?" observed my mum, grappling with her seatbelt.

"That's October for you. We think this new one's in Stradishall?"

"That's what Lesley Dolphin's Facebook said. Remind me where Stradishall is?"

"Over to Bury then off in the general direction of Haverhill," I said.

"Past Ickworth?"

"Yep," I confirmed, "which also had dealings with our mate Capability Brown, I believe."

"Like Hev-e-ning-ham?" garbled my mum.

I snapped her Sunderland-built belt into place. "I thought we'd agreed never to say that name again."

Being more than familiar with the route to Ickworth House from our National Trust trips with the kids, I hadn't scrutinised today's route. Only when we entered Horringer did I realise that this was the cherished A143, albeit the less travelled south-western leg; that made all the difference.

"Your side, soon-ish," I said. "Too new for Street View. That it?" Some white-ish protuberances swished past us. No laybys on the horizon. "Ah, let's stop here. I'm sure they won't mind."

I turned on to a spacious forecourt outside a garage, the type that fixes your car, and parked at maximum distance from the workshop. Central locking plipped, we set off.

"Oi, mate, you can't park there!"

Apparently, they did mind. I held up my hand to the shouty guy in the overalls. "Sorry! Should have asked. I'll move. My fault." No fun being told off as an adult. All was quiet in the Qashqai as I waited to rejoin the flow. On the road again, those same protuberances now slipped by on my side.

"Looks okay by this fence," I said, really not sure if it was okay. "Let's make this quick before they set the dogs on us."

Awkwardly along the verge we tramped, pausing while the occasional HGV roared by. Fortunately, the day was a dry one. Eventually, coast clear, we crossed to **Woodfarm Cottage (#71, Stradishall)** to view a brief run of ivory serpentine topped with pleasingly rounded coping stones. Hundreds of uniquely shaped flints dotted the entire stretch while an undulating length of brown willow fence peeked out over the complete span.

"Basketwork's a bit odd," said my mum, saying it how she saw it. A hand-painted wooden sign on the grass proclaimed this to be the work of Woven Worlds, a "design and build" company run by local craftsman

146

Graham North. His website refers to this structure as a "serpent wall", which I like.

"Obviously not the first wavy wall built this century," I said.

She pondered. "Theberton?"

"To name but one. Ditto Ashbocking, Boyton, etc. Though this is the furthest west we've been."

"Fascinating," said my mum, "but we should check that our transport hasn't been clamped."

Ten minutes later, we were safely back in the motor. Five minutes after that, we were relaxing in the classy and conveniently sited Depden Farm Shop, set back from the bountiful A143. A kickbutt macchiato (on International Coffee Day) and a massive flapjack restored my chemical balance.

~~~~~~~

On the following Tuesday, I biked home to find a fire engine stationed at the end of my road. An unfortunate chap had somehow jumped his BMW over the pavement and destroyed the low garden wall of a house 50m from Broom Acres. That brought to mind the November 2013 incident where an unknown driver demolished part of (what the East Anglian Daily Times referred to as) the "crickle crangle" wall at Easton (#1).

That irresponsible motorist drove off and was never traced; this wasn't an option for the driver on our road who had to be eased out by the fire brigade. I mention this because this was the same unfortunate chap who, eighteen months earlier, had been parking up the road when his foot slipped, so slamming his car into a stationary Renault Grand Scenic: the Broom family Scenic, which was then towed away and written off. Thus appeared the Qashqai, official vehicle of the quest, an emergency purchase from the Nissan garage over the road.

Chapter 29

Through Brome barrelled The Brooms when Mrs Broom notified her husband, Mr Broom, that they'd just passed some bendy bricks.

"You mean the hotel?" I asked.

"No, further on," said my wife.

"Let's check," I said, taking a left into a handy Gulf petrol station called The Devil's Handbasin. That name most likely springs from a nearby plague stone, i.e. the base of a cross once filled with vinegar and used to sanitise germ-ridden medieval coins. Pulling out onto the A140 again, we went past The Swan. Damn your eyes, she was right. There stood **Oak Tua Cottage (#72, Brome)** – that moniker remains a mystery – with its very own dinky run of twenty-brick-tall serpentine. Terracotta pots were balanced on top, and small diamond formations of bricks jutted out. Directly in front stood a wonky tree, a yellow hydrant marker, and a telegraph pole.

Probably built in the last 30 years, it forms a cute Brome triangle – don't go too near – with The Grange (#4) and The Oaksmere (#29).

"Happy?" enquired my wife as we executed another U-turn.

"Very. Half-two and we're already one up. Gonna rack 'em up today."

No need to tell you which road we then took to Beccles where, amid all the crinkle-crankle kerfuffle of the last year, I'd forgotten that Dr Bettley had identified a handful of specimens.

~~~~~~~

Around 3pm we parked at the quay (Google review: "My mate Dave said it's a good place to park your car and if it's good enough for Dave it's good enough for you") and crossed the Waveney to follow never-ending Northgate into town. We entered Puddingmoor – what a name – the road that hugs the river. Right, Waveney House Hotel, left, huge church-yard wall; not that one. Who's this at the foot of the picture-postcard Puddingmoor steps? Why, none other than my mum plus my sister and her son, as arranged.

"Seen it yet?" asked li'l sis.

"Nope. You?"

"Nor us."

"Eyes peeled, crew member six", I said to my nephew.

On we processed. Still no wall. Did see an intriguing sign to the Outdoor Heated Swimming Pool – that'd be Beccles Lido – and the Big Dog Ferry which can transport you to the Geldeston Locks inn three miles away.

Prone to flooding, Puddingmoor overflows with history. We passed places once inhabited by rogues such as James Howell ("will steal anything that comes his way") and Rats Pitchers ("a great drunkard, poacher and suspicious character"); 1859 character sketches courtesy of Mr Harding, Inspector of Police. One or both of these scoundrels may have been im-plicated in the alleged duck stealing of 1872.

"Long and winding road, isn't it?" I said.

"There, finally!" said my nephew, clearly enjoying the family outing.

Opposite the lane to Beccles Rowing Club stands what the *Beccles Conservation Area Character Appraisal* describes as "a row of single storey cottages with only roofs visible behind a wonderful curved crin-kle-crankle wall". Here, at long last, was "the Suffolk undulating brick wall" mentioned by Pevsner at **Puddingmoor (#73, Beccles)**.

Those houses are relatively undistinguished and "much rebuilt" whereas the wall's seen them rise and fall, a chunky relic of things past with a gateway to each property interrupting the flow. It's marked in typical wiggly fashion on the 1884 OS Map near the ancient St Mary's Chapel & Hospital.

"Super," I said. "Two down."

"Two?" asked my mother, taking the bait.

"I'm hungry," said my purple-fleeced nephew.

150

"For more pudding?" I asked. His young face screwed up. "No matter. Remember the fun we had in Sudbury, young Padawan? One more to do."

"Mum?"

My sister smiled. "Whatever your heartless uncle says."

Up Cliff House Steps, nephew now racing ahead, then along Ballygate and into a road marked "access only".

"Isn't this where…," said my mum. I pointed right and made a fishy hand. "Knew it!" she said, pulling out her phone for another picture of the Hungate Lane wall (#11), majestic in the autumnal damp. "Didn't we do this last Christmas with the girls?" I nodded.

"Here's a cafe," suggested my one-track nephew. "And a Gregg's." We carried on. "Don't you want to stop, Nana?" Clever move, kid.

Five minutes to Station Road then a walkway leading to a magnificent view of the Tesco superstore that replaced the William Clowes printing works. Our multigenerational party gathered in an unlovely pavement-less road, hemmed in by a car park fence and backyard walls.

A short stroll to our right found us by the Caxton Club (founded 1890) with its lonely remnant of 6ft crinkle-crankle on **Gaol Lane (#74, Beccles)**. It's possible to train blackberries and blueberries to grow on a hot wall. Rather than soft fruits, these smooth inner curves were graced by two pairs of black and blue wheely bins, attractively chained to the masonry.

"This it with those horrible bins?" said my mum. "Suppose I should take a snap."

Older maps indicate this as all that remains of the southern perimeter of a bowling green – the Beccles Caxton Bowls Club could be seen slightly further along the lane – and that it sat next door to the police station, a landmark that would have been familiar to James Howell and Rats Pitchers.

"Nephew, I'm done. Who's for a bun?"

On Smallgate, opposite Beales department store displaying its vintage gold Beccles Co-operative Society lettering, we found The Galley Cook-shop still happy to serve us at 4:15pm. Chocolate cake for grandmother and grandson, tea and scones for the generation in-between, to celebrate a slew of sightings.

Half-five, husband and wife in the car, and nearly back from Beccles.

"Through Woodbridge?" I asked, innocent as a new-born. She nodded. Up Melton Hill by the redundant council offices, then I indicated right.

"What's down here?"

"That," I announced, stating the obvious now that we were alongside, "is the minty fresh wavy wall on **Pytches Road (#75, Melton)**. Ain't it a honey?"

Innovative Andy had recently emailed me some homemade dashcam footage of this very road showing this pristine brickwork. A big board announced this as The Cedars, "An Exclusive Collection of Individually Designed Executive Family Homes". Woodbridge, never change.

Quality job, too. As the wall turns a corner, the coping stones step down to preserve the height. Four traffic cones seemed unlikely to dissuade the proles from touching the precious wall.

"Sure that's it for today?" she asked.

"Oh yes. Bumper crop. Max walls!"

Chapter 30

My kids used to love a BBC programme called *Deadly 60*. First shown in 2009, the series followed naturalist Steve Backshall as he tracked down three score of the most lethal animals on the planet. We all winced as fearless Steve ventured into a nightmarish cave in Borneo and lifted cockroach-covered rocks in search of the "quite venomous" scutigera. When The Boy asked if he could splash some pocket money on the glossy tie-in trading cards, pound-a-packet, I was all for it. There turned out to be 165 cards to collect, and boy did we collect: got, got, need. Ingeniously, about 120 were "common" (e.g. the paralysis tick), 30 were "rare" (e.g. the lace monitor), and a dozen were "super rare" (e.g. tooth-ragged shark). Father and son became as hooked as a hooked-nosed sea snake, "five times more potent than a cobra". Completing the set became, well, a quest.

While Steve stalked black mambas and reticulated pythons, I had my own serpents to suss out. Despite much recent progress, my online map of known walls in Suffolk – a yellow spot for visited, otherwise red – sported freckles between Wattisfield (#69) to the SW and Redgrave (#50) to the NE. None of these could obviously be classified as "common", i.e. visible to the general public.

Ever onward, I thought we'd attempt another Darsham Cottage (#58) style doorstep challenge and drove the mile-and-a-half to my mum's.

"You're on time? Must be due to that hour we lost last night," she said.

"Possibly. 100th anniversary of the clock change today, did you know?"

"Really?"

"That first one must have been weird," I said. "What was it like?"

"Cheeky. Anyway, where are we going?"

"North. Always north. Allons-y."

Stoke Ash, Thornham Walks and Gislingham went by on our journey up to the cherished A143.

"Townhouse Lane," I pointed out. "This way, Hinderclay." If you're thinking 'Ah, that must have something to do with the clay in those parts,' then give yourself a house point. Then take it away since that's coincidental: the name derives from 'Hildric's clearing'.

"New one to me," said my mum. "A mile out of town and we could be absolutely anywhere."

A single-track road cut between open fields and the odd bungalow, then the houses ceased, placing us in a very Suffolk scene of not a lot. At last came the dead-end on the left that I'd previewed on Google Maps.

"We'll pull over here and walk down that driveway. Nobody around to shout at us today."

After a straight run, our path bent round to give us a view of **Hinderclay Rectory (#76, private)** and its owners, busy with trowels and kneelers.

"Hello!" I said, making my customary introductions. In my head, I sounded like an alien saying take me to your leader.

"Our wall?" said the smiling woman in her green gardening gloves. "Of course. We had somebody asking about it, what…?"

"Maybe ten years ago," completed the man. He gestured. "Here she is."

The official Historic England listing is titled "The Old Rectory with attached crinkle-crankle wall"; I'd reverse those two entities. Their throw-away final sentence cites a wall "about 30m long and 2-3m high". In good shape, it slithered away to the house. Parts of the wall were obscured by clinging greenery mixed with vivid crimson, a treat for the visually impaired.

"Is that Virginia creeper?" asked my mum.

"Oh yes," said Mr Hinderclay. "It does that in the autumn."

This impressive wall probably has its origins in the early C19 enlargement of the timber-framed rectory that's situated a full mile from St Peter's church. A local tale has it that one vicar was given a donkey but missed the sermon when he discovered that it was lame. Leonard A. Gilbert, rector from 1930, took no such chances and purchased a Renault Type AX two-seater (still on the road) to facilitate his journey. Thirty years earlier the same post was held by distinguished antiquarian Edmund Farrer: perhaps you're familiar with his 1908 book, *Portraits in Suffolk Houses (West)*?

GMT light leaving us, we left the hospitable Hinderclay duo to their horticultural chores. "I'd say let's get a cuppa but it's gone four on a Sunday," said my mum.

"Best shift your feet, then," I said, and punched in the second postcode of the day. By the village hall we caught sight of the village sign showing church, windmill and the "gotch", a two-gallon pitcher (inscribed "to be fild with strong beer") for the refreshment of thirsty bell-ringers. The original can be seen at Bury St Edmund's in Moyse's Hall Museum. We were able to slake our thirsts in the soulless interior of the Diss branch of Costa Coffee, open until 5pm. Good lemon muffin, though.

"You know we're in Norfolk?" asked my mum.

"We're not. Are we?"

Chapter 31

With Hinderclay struck off – one less freckle – a handful persisted on Eldest's original list. Two months into her laser-powered career and, with the big man Peter in tow, she'd returned to Broom Acres for our ritual Bonfire Night revelries.

That Saturday morning, I acted as Nespresso wrangler. "A fine day for crinkle-crankling, eh?" I said between shots.

"Very much so," said Peter, who'd done Dunwich (#48) and was keen as a bean. "You coming?" he asked The Boy, sweatily returned from bad-minton practice, who took a big swig from his water bottle and laughed.

"I'd love to come along," said my wife, "but there's around fifteen people due here tonight and someone's got to cook."

"Nana joining us?" asked Eldest.

"Naturally. Oh, and fetch us your list from the fridge, please," which she did. "This particular one – Kessingland, Grove House – has been taxing me for months. You must have seen it in the original Pevsner. Far as I can tell, Grove House is no more. Their parish council didn't answer my emails, but I've made a breakthrough thanks to some helpful librarians up there."

"Fascinating, father. I will have that coffee, thanks," deadpanned my darling daughter.

~~~~~~~

All too predictably the November afternoon was retreating by the time we swished past the giant wind turbine on the A12. At the next roundabout, I fought the urge to carry on to Lowestoft and instead took the third exit. Nana's nattering continued as we parked outside the nearby pub.

"Cool!" said Eldest, suddenly enthused by various signs.

"Can we go in?"

Adjacent to the pub was the entrance to Africa Alive! where they offer an entire (non-deadly) animal alphabet from aardvarks to zebras. An advert on p36 of my retro *Lowestoft & Oulton Broad* pamphlet refers to this as Suffolk Wild Life and Country Park, at that time appealing to tourists with its "British and foreign animals". I noted that p62 had a half-page ad for a "fine Georgian mansion" called Heveningham Hall, open from April to October. Admission to park, garden and house, "subject to revision for 1973", was 20p. Returning to Kessingland in 2016, the largest hoarding featured a rhino to the left and a lion to the right, which, if those creatures were swapped, could be great for teaching relative directions.

"Think they're about to close," I said. "No, we're here for this."

Flanking the zoo's driveway were two brick pillars both joined to stubby bits of wall **(White's Lane, Kessingland, #77)**. The nearest bit – it'd be a stretch to call it a stretch – crinkled and crankled. Just.

"All this way for that?" exclaimed my up-for-the-quest mother.

"Yep. My guess is this is all that's left."

One of the librarians had directed me to a guy called Gerald Brown, and Gerald's wife had told me over the phone that Grove House ("has ribbon wall" wrote Norman Scarfe in his 1960 *Shell Guide*) had morphed into this pub, Livingstone's.

"Look," I said, pointing to a blackboard on the verge. "Chase the ace every Friday. Cash money to be won. What's not to like?"

"I think," said Peter, "this wall is one for the strict enthusiast."

"Deffo. And the good news is that we can walk to the next one."

On the other side of busy White's Lane, we briefly stopped to examine the Kessingland village sign, somewhat symbolically overloaded with (inhale) sun, fish, net, ship's wheel, bell, scythe, sickle, boat, anchor, and three crowns. Three of us walked comfortably under a curious "Residential Area" sign to bring us into **Heritage Green (#78, Kessingland)**. Snaking away from us was a modern wall, neatly stepped as it reduced in height and constructed from fiery red bricks. I snapped away, spun around and saw another twister directly opposite at the entrance to Ark Close. Note that the 1884 OS map shows something called Noah's Ark (?) to the north of The Grove where there's no indication of a wall. Clearly these estate developers built these new walls two-by-two.

"These are better than that first pathetic one," said my mum. To be fair, the ruddy sine waves went well against the golden leaves scattered on the damp tarmac.

"They all count, Nana," said Eldest.

"Well said," I said. "Back to the motor."

Exiting Livingstone's car park, I coasted along White's Lane. "Mind the road!" shouted my mum as I gazed up at a brutal water tower set back on the driver's side.

"Yonder," I said, pulling into **Badger's Holt (#79, Kessingland)**, a new-ish cul-de-sac with a Midsomer Murders name. Here was yet another young pretender, perhaps 25 years old, 2m tall and with an off-white tinge to its lower half. Starts by the house on the corner, executes a couple of shimmies, then finishes by the garage, over and out. A further BOGOF example faces White's Lane itself. Not gonna count that since they're so close.

Still not quite finished – are we ever? – I followed the final tip-off from my whistle-blower and drove up Church Road to The Avenue. We alighted to examine an extended bendy wall facing the playground.

"Surely this is more like it?" said Peter.

I considered. "No. Too far between the curves." Judge and jury, me.

You can't visit this "once-thriving fishing village" (Dr Bettley) without walking on the shingle. Who knew when landlocked Eldest and partner might see the mighty German Ocean again? We managed five windswept minutes before seeking refuge in the Qashqai.

"We should head back and help your mum," I said to my passengers. "Unless The Shed cafe at Henstead is still open?"

It'll be closed, I thought. It was closed. No cake for us. That evening, Broom Acres slowly filled with friends and neighbours – and crew member 6, my orange-fleeced nephew – for pulled pork, Boston beans, and some irresponsible firework fun.

Chapter 32

A few days after Aldi's "54 Shot Big Show" brought a cacophonous end to our pyrotechnics, the fireworks continued further afield as a 70-year-old reality TV celebrity unexpectedly became leader of the free world. His campaign included a promise to "build the wall". Been done already, mate, at Stradishall (#71).

I was puffing up Valley Road a week later when a text pinged in from ping-pong Andy:

Another drunken wall not on your list?

As per his Melton (#75) tip-off, he'd gone full multimedia, attaching eleven key seconds filmed in Debach, Suffolk. Compare and contrast the twenty-six key seconds filmed in Dallas, Texas by Abraham Zapruder, both taken on a Friday morning in November.

~~~~~~~

"What a surprise!" said my mum, clad in a sensible navy blue padded coat, seeing that the Qashqai's front seat was occupied. "I'll take the back."

"Nice to see you too," said my wife. "There's loose talk of lunch. Plus The Boy's at work again."

"He's done well. Must be a wall en route to wherever?"

"Indubitably," I said.

A quarter of an hour later we passed Otley College, home of agriculture, horticulture and bricklaying, then on through Clopton and into Debach.

"Debbitch?" I asked, "like, er, Norman Tebbitch?"

"I'd say Debbidge," said my mum, "like, um, Mary, Mungo and Midge."

"We're looking for some spaced out trees behind a low wall."

"We've run out of houses," said my wife.

"Hold it. Any minute. There."

Intermittently visible through the branches and set way back from the road stood the strikingly symmetrical **Moat House (#80, Debach)**. I pulled over.

"This is someone's driveway," said my wife. "You can't stop here."

"You should come with us more often," I said. "We'll be two minutes. Coming?" I asked my mum.

"We'll be quick," she reassured my wife.

As we'd done at Stradishall, we crabbed along a thin green strip that nobody would classify as pavement. We crossed a straight gravel driveway – the neighbour's? – bordered by an equally straight wall, off which ran a generous stretch of delicately curving crinkle-crankle incorporating an elegant archway. The exemplary lawn that lay between us and those bricks turned everything into guesswork: the wall was maybe 25m long, maybe 3m tall, and of an unknown age.

Originally the rectory for nearby All Saints Church, Moat House, now listed, is shown on an 1887 "Suffolk Sheet" map with a footbridge to the east and an undulating line to the west, presumably our wall. By 1958 it's become The Old Rectory. Now there's a smartly engraved sign on the Coney Weston-esque gateway giving its current name. Why? Well, 2010 excavations uncovered "two surviving arms" of a moat, "both wet".

"Andy did well to spot that," I said, returning to the car. "Those waves wouldn't knock over a sandcastle."

"Agreed," said my mum from some distance behind.

"You said two minutes," observed my wife. "Can we go now?"

"When mum arrives."

The back door opened. "Where's lunch?" asked the dark blue coat.

"Clue: it has a Norwich postcode. Hope you had a big breakfast."

~~~~~~~

We were drawing lots to see who to eat first when I steered off Toad Row into the Henstead Arts & Crafts Centre. Surely The Shed cafe wouldn't deny me thrice? "Open" said a sign, and we three piled in for our late lunch. Tasty toastie for me with turkey, stuffing and cranberry. I couldn't help staring at the red pushbike suspended from the ceiling.

"There's a reason we've come this far?" asked my mum as she dispatched a diet-tomorrow slice of buttered fruit cake.

"Oh, yes," I said in my best Derek Guyler voice. "Another easy one to tick off. From an anonymous source."

Well, nearly. One "John S" had recently emailed me:

There's a small crinkle crankle wall on Richard Crampton Road in Beccles, Suffolk. Hope this helps!

Succinct, John's message, and a great example: get in, get out, don't overstay your welcome.

We duly drove over the Lowestoft railway line into the bottom bit of Beccles, a good mile south of Puddingmoor (#73), and into **Richard Crampton Road (#81, Beccles),** a modern development of bungalows: aim low, they're riding Shetlands. As the road curved away, so did a brief run of contemporary wavy wall that started at a double garage, snaked in and out twice, then terminated. Crimson skirt, me-height, and slowly disappearing beneath a bushy tidal wave.

"Richard Crampton. Didn't he write the Just William books?" I asked as we strolled from alpha to omega and back.

"Close," said my mum.

Opposite was Will Rede Close, the ideal address for a sub-editor's semi-detached. Both Richard Crampton and Will Rede were big in Beccles in the 16th century; the latter is recorded as being the first lord of the manor.

~~~~~~~

The weak November light had dwindled when we returned to Ipswich. Warming the Nutella jar on the toaster was The Boy.

"How was the world of retail?" enquired his mother.

"Fine," he said. "Except I locked my bike on Lloyds Avenue before work. Wasn't there when I got back. I've just walked home."

Despite Suffolk Constabulary's equivalent of The Warren Commission, crime reference SC27112016-286 remains a cold case.

Chapter 33

Long year, short review.

Starting at Boxford (#14) in chilly January and finishing at Beccles (#81) in chilly November, I'd visited 68 distinct Suffolk crinkle-crankle walls. My mum and I had woven from Bacton to Bardwell to Barsham and from Framlingham to Martlesham to Rendlesham, an annus undulatis. That was that for 2016. Or was it?

Every scout hall and church seemed to be advertising a festive event. Around Yoxford we'd noticed some roadside posters for a Christmas market at a little place called Heveningham Hall. Will, my contact there – not The Man From Del Monte – had mentioned their summer country fair but not a winter equivalent. The event's sleek website promised handmade pies, live reindeer and free entry; nothing about the gardens.

Since this wasn't going to be the usual magical mystery tour, my wife did the driving including the obligatory maternal pick-up.

"Front seat's yours," I said.

"Ta," said my mum, unhesitatingly. "Heveningham Hall, please, driver," she continued, mangling that first word.

"Right you are," said my wife.

"You won't see their wall, you know," added my mum.

"He who dares, mother."

Soon we were passing Helmingham Hall – "Wrong one," pointed out my mum – then our chauffeuse eventually signalled right and, waddya know, we'd crossed into the sacred grounds of Heveningham Hall. My, what a pile. We joined many other cars on the grass and, lured by the smell of roasting chestnuts, walked up to the action on the right of the big house. Every other male was wearing a Santa suit; there'd been a fun run that morning. Noticing that the stalls formed a U-shape, I realised that we stood within the horseshoe-shaped stables designed by – checks notes – one Capability Brown.

While the womenfolk inspected the merchandise, I slipped away and sidled around the block. Due south of me, perhaps 100m away, sadly screened by a conspiracy of mature trees, lay a walled kitchen garden dating from 1720.

Ten metres further on, the stables all but behind me, I heard some dogs begin to bark and pictured being on the wrong end of Mr Hunt's hounds. That was enough for a rapid about-turn.

"Any joy?" asked my mum.

"Nope. So near and yet so far."

~ 2017 ~

~ 2017 ~

Chapter 34

New year, old walls.

Following 2016's efforts, my to-do list had shrunk like a cashmere sweater in a hot wash. Three entries, all fished from my original trawl of the Historic England website, were, weirdly, clumped in one village – Rickinghall. Near Diss, it comprises two parishes, Rickinghall Superior and Rickinghall Inferior, St Mary's at RS being higher than St Mary's at RI. The latter parish included walls at Brook House, Broom Hills and Snape Hill House.

We'd been thereabouts on earlier forays to Hinderclay (#76) and Botesdale (#52) without spying any of this trio. While the two Hills were relatively remote, Brook House faced the lower church. Aerial images revealed no curves, and, on our perambulations, a neighbour mentioned extensive recent building work. Aware that not all edifices survive (the owner of Easton (#1) can attest to the cost of proper repairs) I reluctantly removed Brook House from my list. That same resident provided a surname for one of the Hills; that name appeared online with contact details which I forwarded to myself: Rickinghall, don't lose that number.

After negotiations, the owner agreed to a visit in early January on one particular condition.

"Tomorrow afternoon," I informed my mum, "can you bring some form of ID? After all, we could be anybody."

"You could be anybody! Fine, I'll find something."

~~~~~~

At 2:25pm I turned off The Street by The Rickinghalls' two-faced village sign, one side clearly Superior, the other obviously Inferior, into Hinderclay Road. We ignored Mill Lane and instead took a long gravel drive-way to **Snape Hill House (#82, Rickinghall, private)**. Miscellaneous outbuildings greeted us, as did a smiling woman.

"You found us," she said as we walked over. "I'm Sue."

"And this is me," I said, waving my driving licence while my mum rifled through her handbag.

"Oh, I don't need that. Shall we?"

Across a yard, through a gate, and we beheld a serpentine leviathan: 4m tall, 40m long, says Historic England. Imagine the hods to carry those bricks. Elegant individual bay trees, their tips level with the top of the massive windbreak, occupied the inner curves, each planted in those hefty ceramic pots that you absolutely believe you can carry from the garden centre to your car. Devoid of other greenery, that brickwork felt naked and better for it.

"That's a size," commented my mum.

"Impressive," I added.

"Glad you like it," said Sue. "Would you care to see the other one?"

"There's another one?" said mother and son.

"Yes," said Sue, guiding us around the superstructure, "though somewhat less grand."

Hidden from the formal grandeur of the lawn ran an eccentric half-height crinkle-crankle supported by chunky buttresses as if it lacked the confidence of its older brother. Those stretcher bricks seemed paler too.

We focused on the garden rather than the three-storey white house, originally known as plain Hill House. Around 1820, a likely date for the leviathan, the Amys family carried out major works and split the grand house from nearby Snape Farm, "Snape" meaning a boggy piece of land. There are prehistoric clay pits in Rickinghall, according to Historic England: lot of clay, lot of potters.

"We'll take some photos if that's OK," I said, "and be off."

"Absolutely," said Sue, and by 3pm we were occupying a prime spot outside the village Co-op, comparing snaps and sipping bottles of Tropicana made all the sweeter for finally ticking off a Rickinghall wall.

Chapter 35

As the quest progressed, I'd realised that the size of my to-do list, much like your investment's value, could go up as well as down. Ask people to keep you posted and they just might do that.

In pursuit of Grove House (#77), I'd been helped by "a woman from Kessingland library" whose name then evaporated. That same librarian – Jill Walker – had now emailed me seven bullet points, each being the verified location of a crinkle-crankle wall. Jill and colleagues had been busy on my behalf "making notes as we travelled around". Librarians are the best.

Keen for my own list not to double in size, I scanned those bullets hard: eliminating those already seen still left a quartet to check out, all in Carlton Colville, home to a fine example at The Old Rectory (#46). This fresh batch was concentrated in a modern development. Visiting those would require neither prior permission nor proof of identity.

With Eldest living and working away, Middler at university, The Boy working and my wife largely indifferent, the dependable duo drove one hour north on a dreich January afternoon.

First stop was "in the vicinity of the play area on **Deepdale**" (#83, **Carlton Colville**), a name familiar from my father-in-law's boyhood adoration of Preston North End. "Up the hill on your right" advised Jill, where we found two uniformly coloured in-and-outs squashed behind a green lamp post and dwarfed by the six-bedroom three-floor house opposite.

"Yes, that's it," I said.

I executed a three-point turn and put the wipers back on as we passed Coplow Dale, Nidderdale, then into **Colsterdale (#84, Carlton Colville)**. Slightly more subtle curves on this one, slightly longer, no lamp post, and as unremarkable as the anonymous bungalow it faced.

"Is everywhere a dale here?" asked my mum.

"All Yorkshire Dales, I think."

Ten minutes in, two walls done. Not the same thrill of the chase resulting from the months spent trying to pin down Snape Hill House, say. Jill's next suggestion took us north over the A1145.

In **Ashburnham Way (#85, Carlton Colville)**, she said, "there are at least a couple". Finding a free kerb in Elm Coppice, I noticed we'd swapped dales for trees.

"See it?" I asked.

"Course!"

"Back this way."

"No, over there," insisted my mum.

We crossed to examine the really rather lengthy stretch of at least ten bumps that I'd contrived to miss. While I took souvenir snaps, my mum marched along the damp pavement as if inspecting the troops.

"Two sections," she observed, "one taller than the other. Bit odd."

"And there's my short segment," I pointed out.

I briefly stood on the dotted white line. I'd looked at walls from both sides now. My shorter example weaved away behind some ornamental bushes only to reappear down the road. Jill was dead right: there were indeed "at least a couple" here.

"Right," I said, "that's enough examples. I need a fix. Let's skedaddle."

I signalled right so that we could take in the rest of Ashburnham Way. Another wavy wall appeared on our left and bent around the corner into Elmdale Drive – note that tree plus dale portmanteau – then we saw one more stretch followed by a much longer section, and on, and on, and on.

"Dozens of the blighters," I said. "Devalues the whole enterprise. This one road must have the most bendy walls in Suffolk."

"Carlton Colville," said my mum, "is crinkle-crankle central."

~~~~~~~

To Starbucks on the Lowestoft high street for a perfectly fine jug of latte before returning to base where Google located an East Suffolk planning application. A resident of Ashburnham Way wanted to increase the height of their boundary wall:

> *The distinctive wavy form of the wall is characteristic of the locality and was a deliberate design feature when this large, phased housing development was planned in the early 1980s with the aim of adding variety to the built form... as a means of preventing the streetscape from appearing bland and repetitive. The applicant is to be applauded for recognising and appreciating the public benefit of retaining this design feature, rather than simply requesting to replace it entirely with a new straight wall or fence which would have been a much cheaper option...*

Long live variety of the built form!

Chapter 36

Prior to the quest I knew bupkis about Brampton. Now I know it's equidistant from Beccles and Southwold, and that, should I feel the need, I could catch a direct train there from Ipswich. I'd need to mention my intended destination to the conductor, though, since it's a request stop on the line to Lowestoft.

That village had been bubbling away in my cerebellum for over a year, ever since Edward Martin of the Suffolk Institute of Archaeology had cited Brampton Hall. Getting nothing from the net, we'd swung by in the summer and stopped by the "fairly vicious bend" (says Simon Knott) on which the church of St Peter stands, the hall being the former rectory. An amble through the graveyard abutting the house yielded zilch. Ditto when I peeked down the driveway.

My analogue mother sent a quizzical letter to the unknown owners giving my contact details. They responded with a large font six-word email:

"We have no crinkle crankle walls"

I replied, asking if an old wall might have fallen down or been removed, and was rewarded with a further seven words:

"Could this be at Brampton Old Hall?"

And that split the case wide open. Still nothing online about an old wall at the old hall but a speculative phone call to a local artist came up trumps.

"Yes," said Brampton-based printmaker Ni Gooding, "there's a wavy wall there. It's on a public footpath so you can walk right past it." Nice one, Ni.

~~~~~~~

Was wet and windy when we pulled over on Station Road by a teardrop-shaped parcel of grass, closer to Redisham than Brampton. Two modest properties overlooked the green. Of more interest to mother and son was the grander property already visible at the end of the tree-lined avenue to our right.

"OK to go down here, you reckon?" asked my mum, zipping her coat.

"There's the bridleway sign," I said. "That should show us the way."

Short of the white brick **Brampton Old Hall (#86)**, "remodelled in the C19 in C16 style" says Dr Bettley, our path cut left, as did we.

"There she blows," I said. A waist-high wall wiggled away from us and, after gaining some traction, shot up to double its original height. Furry green patches veiled the top of the lower section.

"All those mossy bits," said my mum.

"Trouble with tribbles," I said. "I'll explain later."

We followed it around the corner. Its elevation meant that we couldn't gawp into the hall's back garden. When it ended, we couldn't help but notice a sizeable white marquee on the lawn.

"What's that about?" wondered my mum.

"Search me."

The 1883 map denotes this location as Brampton Hall - Edward Martin was right – complete with multiple moats. Within 40 years it's been rebranded as Brampton Old Hall, having ceded its title to the property near the bend. Quarter of an hour later, appreciating the solidity of the roof and walls of Coffeelink at Darsham, I fired up the 4G.

"Ah," I said, "remember Jim Prior?"

"I do," said my tea-pouring mother. "MP for Lowestoft? Ruddy face?"

"Yep, him. In Thatcher's cabinet. Evidently he became Baron Prior of Brampton. The Old Hall was his home."

"Interesting. And the tent?"

"Oh." I read on. "Says he died before Christmas. The memorial service was two days ago followed by 'a celebration at the family home', according to the East Anglian Daily Times."

"Didn't know that. But this brownie's good."

176

Chapter 37

In December we'd had a rare if welcome visit from my cousin Martin and his family. I grew up in west Ipswich; my uncle and aunt (and their two sons) lived on the other side of town, an unfathomably long distance when you're six years old. For the past few years Martin had been resident somewhat further away, in Tasmania. Catching up - we hadn't exactly seen much of each other in the previous 30 years - I must have mentioned the quest, hence his Christmas Eve email:

> "I may have come across another wall for you. It appears to be at a second location in Boxford. The one you have is Church St. This is Swan St."

Super, I thought: yet another one to do.

~~~~~~~

My darling daughters were home for the last weekend of February.

"What's the plan?" asked Eldest late on Saturday morning as she struggled to bisect a bagel.

"Got a wall to tick off. All set up with Nana."

"That's the best we can do?" said Middler.

"Yep. Mum's in too."

"Am I?" said my wife, nervously watching the bread knife.

~~~~~~~

By 1:30pm four paid-up members of the crinkle-crankle crew (plus my wife) were cruising past Hadleigh before parking on Broad Street, opposite the Fleece Inn in jigsaw-worthy Boxford. "Very nice," said my wife, admiring two oddly placed Gothick arches by the phone box.

"Lovely," said Eldest. "Those little bridges over the river are cute."

"See that motorbike on the village sign?" I said. "That's because-"

"Yeah, you told us," said Middler.

"Always a joy to be out with the fam," I continued. "Follow me."

I steered them away from the centre and into Swan Street where, in turn, we admired Old Castle House, Victoria Cottage and Kingsbury House with their respective cross-wings, glazing bars and ornamental fanlights. All was quiet at number 33, the target property.

"I'm going into the butcher's to ask." Two minutes later, I emerged.

"Any news?" asked my blue-fleeced mum.

"Chap had never heard the term crinkle-crankle. And when I described it said there's no such thing round here. Except we've already seen that one round the corner on Church Street (#14). Let's walk a bit further."

As I'd foreseen on Street View, a lane edged between the houses on our left. "Up here." Left again was a dead-end track with a handful of parking spaces and access to the rear of **Swan Street (#87, Boxford, private)**.

"Worth a poke," I said, setting off.

"I'm staying here," said my wife.

"I'll join you if no one else will," said my mother, ever game.

Tucked behind a purple-ish picket fence, we found an eighteen-brick tall serpentine dividing two small terrace gardens. Both houses, numbers 31 and 33, are listed – "timber-framed and plastered" – albeit with no mention of the wall. Decidedly not new, it's hard to date.

"That's quite a few crinkles. Or crankles. I never know which is which," said my mum.

"Yep. Short and wiggly. Quick snap then we'll rejoin the others."

"You could live your whole life in Boxford and not know this was there," said my mum.

Martin's email had ended with "if correct, I would appreciate a spotter's badge." Cousin, I'll hand that over next time you're in town.

Chapter 38

Ledbury, Leominster and Ludlow are all undoubtedly lovely. Closer to home, "there is nothing in Suffolk to compete with the timber-framed houses of Lavenham," wrote Pevsner. That may be, Nikolaus, but the Wallfinder General (and his mother) were less interested in the remarkable carved medieval bressummers behind us and more interested in the unremarkable Victorian terrace before us.

"Half-five," I said, and rung the bell.

Rightmove had done a fine job of revealing under the radar serpentines from Hollesley (#41) to Halesworth (#59) and had now flagged up an example in the 14th wealthiest town in England; well, that was the case in 1524. Up for grabs was **The Old Manse (#88, Lavenham, private)**, a four-bed country house with "gardens enclosed by brick walls including a section of Georgian crinkle-crankle wall which is particularly impressive". Yours, with five grand change, for a million quid.

On a previous visit to Barn Street nobody had answered my rat-a-tat on the Manse door: for all I knew it was vacant. Compensation had arrived up the road in the National Trust cafe in The Guildhall which served the best scone I'd ever tasted. I'm still sampling baked goods far and wide – someone's got to do it – and have yet to find its equal. Where were we?

Scouring Rightmove sometime later, I found a more modest property, a two-bed terrace on Water Street, named for its alignment to a stream that once fed the ponds at Lavenham Hall. To the rear of this relatively affordable house, "the right-hand boundary has a wonderful old crinkle-crankle red brick wall" – nice – "adjoining the grounds of The Old Manse". Of course! I really should have known that every wall has two sides.

A message here, a message there, then current owner Tom was kind enough to facilitate a late Friday afternoon visit. He now welcomed us in to one of the redbrick terraces built, according to the plaque sandwiched between the first-floor windows, by W.W. Roper & Sons in 1891. If you're itching to know the source of William Whittingham Roper's money, the answer is horsehair. There's a sample of his men's suit lining at the V&A.

We trampled through Tom's living room and out through the back door to catch the last of the light. There, laid out in Lavenham, was the shared wall.

Gentle bends on this one, the mossy coping stones up to my shoulder and the smooth curves interrupted by some randomly sited birch trees, some in the concave sections, some not. Somewhere over there was The Old Manse: we couldn't really see it thanks to a modern black mesh fence on the far side which snaked along the entire length. Wrapped in clinging greenery, it doubled the height of the wall. What goes on in the Manse stays in the Manse. Were those bricks Georgian? Let's take the agent's word for it.

"Your son tells me you've seen a few of these before?" asked Tom.

"More than a few," answered my mum. "Think we're up in the 80s now. This one's nice."

Before The Old Manse had an extension built in 2012, the boys and girls of Suffolk Archaeology got their trowels out. Their extensive report excludes any reference to the wall but they did find "two large pits" containing much C15/C16 pottery, not quite as exciting as the "tessellated Roman pavement" located nearby by Basil Brown "although its precise location is not known". Much like Norman Scarfe's list of crinkle-crankle walls.

We left Tom to his tea and emerged on to Water Street, beams to the left of us, jetties to the right.

Chapter 39

Cast your mind back to March 1915 and the London opening of *Rosy Rapture*, "a burlesque in seven scenes" by J.M. Barrie. Yes, that one. Among the songs was the tongue-twisting *Which Switch is the Switch, Miss, for Ipswich?* with audience participation encouraged. Now fast-forward to March 2017 and the imminent birthday of Eldest, crew member number two, living in Bedfordshire with 2m Peter. Her wishlist contained a single big-ticket item: a games console, the Nintendo Switch.

"I'll take care of that," I reassured my wife.

With less than 24 hours to go before a cross-county celebration trip, I'd very much failed to take care of that: The Switch was that spring's Tracy Island. My online stock alerts at John Lewis and Tesco resembled church mice. Argos seemed to have their own supply but no sooner had one appeared than it disappeared, most likely to be flipped for a higher price.

"I'll give her the money instead," I said as we walked round to some friends on the Saturday evening.

"Fine, but it's not the same, is it?" replied my eternally spot-on wife.

Slurping San Pellegrino and chatting, I continued to check my phone like an irksome teenager. Ooh, another Argos alert. Three in stock at Braintree. Hang on, that's off the A120, near our route tomorrow. Go to site. One in stock. Add to basket. Pay now. Thank you for your FastTrack order.

"I've got one!" I cried. "I've only gone and got one!"

~~~~~~~

Seven days after the narrator saved the day – aided by his wife's chocolate cake, illuminated by a Stonehenge of candles – 'twas time to switch his attention back to the waning list of wavy walls. Last Sunday, the delights of

Braintree; this Sunday, the charms of Brampton. Yes, there again.

Back when I was a noob and didn't know my Brampton Hall from my Brampton Old Hall, I'd emailed the local parish council clerk, and although Tracey Burrows couldn't help with the halls, she did throw in this mic drop:

"There is also a crinkle-crankle wall at Dog Cottage, London Road"

Given my many new contacts in the village, I was able to locate John (the owner of DC) shortly afterwards. Things then went quiet for several months before John resurfaced to say "visit any time". Unfortunately that was a couple of weeks after we'd visited the Old Hall (#86). On a sunlit Sunday I emailed ahead to say we'd swing by that afternoon.

Approaching the village on the straight A145, the wheaty fields finally stopped and I pulled over by the first house on the left. No other vehicles, nobody at the door, and not a creature stirred under the ornate white bargeboards.

"You sure this is the place?" asked my mum.

"Definitely. Chap said to go through the gate. I say let's do it."

I expected to find a somewhat diminutive structure of the kind we'd seen at Boyton (#31) a year earlier. Not so. **Dog Cottage (#89, Brampton, private)** boasts a chunky six-foot serpentine of half a dozen curves, plus it turns through a right angle. Pretty decent given the champion back story from John:

"Built in the 70s by my father with a section rebuilt in the 2000s" – here comes the kicker – "after our horse knocked it over."

Ivy trailed up some parts, one or two pet graves kept an ominous watch, and a brightly coloured but weather-beaten and slightly creepy wooden figure – a pied piper? – leaned against one of the inners.

Not that big and not in the best condition, advised John. I beg to disagree. If that were running through my back garden, I'd be mighty proud.

~~~~~~~

Further north half an hour later and we were rubbernecking the monster 12ft crinkle-crankle on Garden Lane at Worlingham (#13); we'd been here one dark afternoon in the early days of the crew. That neighbouring bus stop must live in fear of high winds.

"Amazing as this is, it's not what we're here for," I explained to my Motorola-wielding mother. "There's something at the end of the road."

I reparked by the entrance to Grade I Worlingham Hall, "a breath-taking countryside house" available to rent through Airbnb for a breath-taking price, and likely with connections to that huge wall. On a pocket lawn near the gate sat a lonely bench. I gestured to a square concrete base next to it.

"There's literally no sign," I said. "Here's where the village sign should be."

"Vandals? Repair?" suggested my mum.

"Could be. Shame, though, since part of that sign shows that massive wall. Some you win. On we go."

~~~~~~~

We had one final bunch o' bricks to check out, a mile along Lowestoft Road at a new-ish close called **The Walnuts (#90, Worlingham)**. Another Rightmove result, one of the houses had a "garden enclosed by a crinkle-crankle wall".

Probably pre-millennium, it bent sweetly around the corner from the main road into the cul-de-sac and could have teleported here from Carlton Colville. Quite attractive coping, though, those inverted battlements similar to Halesworth (#59), and with a sprinkling of daffs at its base. I'd guess its presence pays homage to its mighty ancestor on Garden Lane.

Attached to a post by the knee-high road sign was a neighbourhood watch sign. Fair play, then, to the curtain-twitching neighbour who watched us nutters with interest as we snapped away at the mundane structure.

"I prefer that one at Dog Cottage," said my mum. I nodded.

Just about time for us to beat last orders at the well-reviewed Tally Ho tearooms in the border village of Mettingham; credit to them for their rare Sundays-until-5pm hours. We mostly enjoyed a peculiarly retro experience with doilies, cake racks, and scones "barely acquainted with the oven", according to my mum.

Then back to the 'Swich.

Chapter 40

Let's start at The Co-op in Rickinghall, a very good place to start.

Head up the access road to The Street, indicate right, and check both ways before pulling out. Accelerate to 25mph then ease off once you spot a cream-coloured house named Cambria through the offside window. Left into Garden House Lane and again into Ryder's Way. Here, you'll snake through a well-kept modern development before coming to a freestanding double garage with a pyramidical tiled roof. That functional structure marks the entrance to Basil Brown Close, an unremarkable road commemorating a remarkable man.

By the way, *Cambria*, that property we passed on The Street, was the Brown family home where he lived with his wife May from 1935.

Born in Bucklesham (east of Ipswich) in 1888, Basil was only a few months old when the family moved 30 miles north to Rickinghall in the northernmost part of Suffolk. He scratched a living as a tenant farmer, insurance agent and special constable, although his two primary interests were astronomy – leading him to publish a book in 1932 – and archaeology – leading to his 1939 discovery of the Anglo-Saxon ship buried at Sutton Hoo. Not bad for someone who left school aged 12.

Basil retired in 1961 having been loosely employed by Ipswich Museum for nearly 30 years. In 1964, however, intrigued by reports of an oddly coloured patch in a nearby field, he started an excavation at a site named Broomhills. He'd eventually find evidence of a pagan manor house and, alas, suffer a stroke or heart attack that finally put an end to his active involvement. Basil died in his cottage in 1977.

~~~~~~~

Forty years later I parked on the driveway of the seven-bay and two-storey **Broomhills (#91, Rickinghall, private)**. There were no obvious spindle whorls or cruciform brooches in sight but my mum was pointing to the start of a fine C19 crinkle-crankle, its end ostentatiously topped with a worn stone pineapple. Or possibly an artichoke.

"Half-five," I said, and knocked on the door.

Each of these final few examples had required much digging and Broomhills was no exception. Owner Sue – not to be confused with Susan over the fields at Snape Hill House – had come good and consented to a Lavenham-esque late afternoon visit. After the usual introductions, Sue gave us a brief tour along the splendid 25m length, taking in the odd arch and change of height, before leaving us to it in the April drizzle. Not quite as tall as Snape Hill, Sue's wall is in no way inferior. That, right there, is a rare Rickinghall pun.

Near a greenhouse halfway down the garden, the wall took a turn, twisting 90 degrees left to form an L-shape. The whole thing made for a fine prospect with shocking red tulips and yellow-green euphorbia penetrating the dour conditions, more so when set against a number of white patches on the brickwork – efflorescence caused by crystalline salts and exaggerated by the damp conditions.

Slightly breaking up the curves were a series of square protrusions as if someone were pushing against the other side: perhaps these were the "inner pilaster strips" mentioned in the Historic England listing?

"Seen enough?" I asked as we wiped our phone screens.

"About five minutes ago," replied my mum.

Basil Brown's excavation on this site ran for five years in the mid-1960s, sandwiching my birthdate. I'd be fascinated to know what he made of the crinkle-crankle phenomenon and this particular wall.

Chapter 41

In *You Need Me, I Don't Need You*, the second single from his 2011 debut album, Yorkshire-born Ed Sheeran gets his sibilance on and sings that "Suffolk sadly seems to suffocate me". This Ed, yours truly, has never felt that way, and while occasional Google searches brought up crinkle-crankles further afield, such as the aforementioned Wheathampstead and West Horsley Place, I brushed them aside: after all, there were still fresh examples – one or two – to tick off here.

However, a one-off event listed online snagged my walleye and reeled me in. Discussions were had, arrangements were made, and, aged 51 years and 7 days, I climbed into the Qashqai cockpit shortly before 10am on a brilliantly sunny Sunday: for the very first time mother and son would cross the county line to view a wavy wall not in the land of the South Folk.

"This is novel," said my mum, clicking in as once advised by Shaw Taylor. "What sort of time do you think we'll get there?"

"About one," I said, "traffic permitting."

~~~~~~~

Traffic did not permit, dear reader – I'm not convinced these so-called "motorways" will catch on – and, having masterfully reversed into a spot by St Andrews C of E church, I saw that its clock said quarter-past-two. We emerged, did the customary service station stretch, and managed the few steps into the porch under some blue & white bunting.

"Are you here for the art show?" asked a cheerful woman by a tea urn.

"Sadly not," I said. "The open gardens?"

"Then you'll need one of these," she said, handing me an A4 sheet entitled *NGS: Headington Gardens*.

"Let's get our bearings," I said to my mum back in the warmth of the afternoon. "We're on St Andrew's Road" – I pointed to a black symbol like a cartoon detonator – "and we're aiming for letters 'h' and 'i' up here."

"Right-o," said my mum.

Heading west on foot, I ran my fingers along a stone wall. The road fittingly curved one way then another before a bright yellow National Garden Scheme hoarding beckoned us into a driveway between orb-topped pillars. My mum scanned a bright white sign planted in the earth.

"Welcome to **Ruskin College**, Oxford. This it?"

"Indeedy. And for once we don't need to knock on the door."

Down a path dwarfed by the college itself, a cube of contemporary academic architecture, and we'd arrived. While my mum walked on, I took my sweet time reading an information board all about "The history and restoration of the Ruskin Crinkle Crankle Garden". Let me borrow its excellent opening para:

"Also known as crinkum-crankum, wavy or crinkle-crankle walls are a way of economising on bricks. They are also good for kitchen gardens as fruit trees can be sheltered within the curves and aligned to face the sun. They are associated with East Anglia..." – I know! – *"although their use has spread to other parts of England and Wales, and possibly dates back to the mid 17th century when Dutch engineers were employed to drain the fens. In the Netherlands the design is called slange muur (snaking wall). Thomas Jefferson used this form in the grounds of the University of Virginia having appreciated both its aesthetic value and economy."*

There's everything you need to know about crinkle-crankle walls but were afraid to ask.

Apparently, the present garden with its solitary south-facing serpentine goes back to C18 and one William Finch. Good to see that, even in the city of dreaming spires, they couldn't date its construction any more precisely than that. Enough with the prevaricating: I strolled past a troop of pink and purple foxgloves to join my mum. She was shaking her head at the looming 3m tall structure.

"All this way and it isn't even a proper crinkle-crankle wall! Those are just straight bits joined at odd angles. Where's the curves?"

She was right: despite both Ruskin College and Heritage England labelling this as crinkle-crankle, it's actually a series of six linear sections, each pair resembling an open wallet. If you recall John Claudius Loudon's 1822 *Encyclopaedia of Gardening*, figure 149 shows "the wavy or serpentine wall" that we know and love; what we were looking at was figure 150, "the angular wall", which, he says, "is recommended on the same general principles of shelter and economy".

"Quality espaliers, though. And the garden itself is coming on."

"Those chives are pretty in the sun," she said. "I'll give you that."

Forty years earlier we'd have been standing on the hard tennis court that sat, like Googie Withers, within these walls. That fell into disrepair in the 1990s, and only in 2009 did the college raise enough money to mount a restoration project. Shortly after that, in tandem with Headington locals, they launched a grow-your-own-veg project called – wait for it – the Crinkle Crankle Club. Close but no cigar. Those tidy terraced beds of green growth all around us were testimony to the club's ongoing work.

After a brief look at the rough white-ish exterior of the angular brick-work, and a sit-down on a handy bench for my be-cardiganed mum, we agreed it was time to take tiffin at the associated Crinkle Crankle Café (actual name) in the base of the academic cube. Cuppa for my mum, frothy coffee for me, and a pair of Tunnock's tea cakes. Huge opportunity lost, we both felt, for serpentine-themed foodstuffs. Ideas on a postcard, please.

Refreshed, I suggested that we check out some of the other open gardens on our sheet. "So long as we don't have to walk too far," insisted my passenger.

~~~~~~~

My word, such primness and poshness at the Coach House and the White Lodge, with their mirrored pyramids, spectacular water features, and regimented topiary.

"There's one more thing I'd like to show you," I said as we neared the busy London Road at the southern extremity of our hand drawn map. "But let's pop in here first for a cold drink to take away."

I held open the door of a conveniently sited Starbucks. Before stepping inside, my mum glanced over her shoulder. "What on earth…?"

The coffee shop faces a side road called New High Street where, at number two, we find *Untitled 1986*, a 25-feet fibreglass sculpture of a shark diving into the tiled roof of an ordinary terraced house.

"Isn't that something? That's the Headington Shark. What do you fancy, juice or a milkshake?"

Chapter 42

Dr James Bettley has been a constant presence since the earliest days of the quest. Let me remind you that he's the "freelance architectural historian" who greatly updated the Pevsner guide to Suffolk, splitting it into East and West volumes (both published 2015), and who'd cranked out a 960-page Essex tome (2007) to boot. In February 2016 I'd been chuffed to swap emails with him where he helpfully listed all of his Suffolk serpentine citations; in response I proudly mentioned the 34 I'd already visited. A month later I was most pleased to receive this:

> *"Just thought you'd like to know that I've spotted, on Google Maps, a crinkle-crankle wall along the NE side of the walled garden at Broke Hall, Nacton. Best wishes, James."*

James: hear that? Not worthy, I'll continue to refer to him as Dr Bettley.

Since then, Broke Hall had occupied a chilly slot on my to-do list while its neighbours thawed and advanced to the ready-to-eat section. As an Ipswich lad, I knew that name from green corporation buses at Tower Ramparts; such a double-decker would be heading in the opposite direction to my Whitehouse number eight. I hadn't appreciated that the Broke Hall estate, north of Foxhall Road, took its name from a grand country house five miles away in the village of Nacton.

Aerial photos showed an unbeatable setting out there on the banks of the River Orwell. The house, I learned, had long since been partitioned into flats and my attempts at establishing contact came to naught. A sign leading to the property's grand tree-lined approach – Private Land, Keep Out – didn't encourage the casual visitor.

Then friend Andy came in handy: he'd scoured his OS maps and showed me a legitimate right of way to the north of the grounds that should permit me a distant view of the brickwork.

~~~~~~~

So, seven days after we went down to Oxford town, I decided to seize the bike by the handlebars and push out to Nacton, a seven-mile trip equivalent to my daily commute. This would be my first quest-related voyage en velo since St Edmund's Road (#26). That had been on my classy Boardman, a machine I'd sadly mislaid. Three weeks earlier I'd cycled into town to catch *Mulholland Drive* at the Film Theatre. When I emerged two hours later, it had vanished like The Boy's bike: less Lynch, more Vittorio De Sica.

Round the buzzy waterfront on my fat-tyred back-up bike, across Holywells Park to the coincidentally named Nacton Road, then fingers crossed at the cycle-hostile A14 junction. Beyond the town were trees, fields, repeat. Finally came an attractive old wall marking the boundary of Orwell Park, a posh prep school complete with its own observatory. Right into Church Road with, at the end, a choice of three routes: not right to Nacton Shores picnic site, not straight to the private driveway, but left along a gravel path in the welcome shade of the woods. Andy reassured me I could go this way, I thought as I dismounted, sipped Lucozade, and pushed my pushbike.

Open grass on the right gave way to assorted smaller estate residences that blocked my view of the big house. Fifty yards further I could finally glimpse a walled garden. I edged closer.

Whoever owns **Broke Hall (#92, Nacton, private)** has themselves a splendid serpentine. Over there was a fancy wooden gate from which snaked a set of tall (2m+) bays, the inner sections filled with log piles. Closer to me the wall dropped half a dozen bricks before sweeping the corner to become perfectly straight on its SE aspect. Satellite images showed a pair of square formal gardens on the other side of that wall. Somebody clearly cares for these grounds, as indeed they should since the park was designed by Humphry Repton, sometimes seen as Capability Brown's successor.

Dr Bettley (never James) tells us that Repton was educated alongside Philip Bowes Broke, for whom the house was remodelled in the early 1800s. Broke's father, also Philip, was MP for Ipswich from 1730-1733.

If you're still with me, Broke's eldest son, yet another Philip, commanded *HMS Shannon* in the War of 1812 and famously captured *USS Chesapeake*.

In later years *HMS Shannon* joined the reserve fleet in Portsmouth and was ultimately dismantled at Chatham in 1859. Relics of the frigate, such as the ship's bell, can still be seen in Nova Scotia if you're out that way. I was reliably informed by Paul, a Nacton resident, that the ornate gate I'd seen in the Broke Hall serpentine is "made from the timbers of *HMS Shannon*".

A life on the ocean wave, a gate in the wavy wall.

Chapter 43

Heveningham, I'm in Heveningham, and my heart beats so…

Underneath her floppy sunhat, my mum (crew member 5) was less concerned with matters cardiac and more with matters gastric. She'd been in the back while my wife Colin McRae'd it along the bendy B1117 and was now trying not to heave on to the grass behind the Qashqai.

"I don't remember feeling car sick before," she managed, her face a similar hue to her white top. "You're OK?"

"Used to it," answered Middler (crew member 3), home for the hols. "That was nothing compared to Italy."

"You should have said something," said my wife, scanning the approach. "Is that them?"

Our quartet watched a tiny black car tootle off the B-road and up the track to be marshalled into a row just down the slope. At the wheel was Eldest (crew member 2) with 2m Peter concertinaed into the passenger seat.

"I'll travel with them next time," muttered my mum.

"Shall we?" I said, nodding towards the desk and unfolding our £14 adult tickets to the 2017 Brigadoon Country Fair. Half-twelve and we'd already missed the Spitfire flypast. Queue, scan, enter: the narrator (crew member 1 and, according to my badge, leader of the CCC) had finally been legitimately admitted, along with hundreds of other folk, to the glorious grounds of **Heveningham Hall (#93, private)**. Up on the left stood "the only house in Suffolk really worth seeing", the verdict of Francois de la Rochefoucauld after his 1784 tour of the county. Out of bounds today, it wasn't what I'd come for.

"There's a wall I very much need to see," I announced, setting off in my middle-aisle sandals. The shortest of strolls around Capability Brown's stable block would lead us to the "walled garden of c1720" (thanks, Dr Bettley), allegedly constructed with bricks from the original house.

"We're all coming," said my mostly recovered mum.

Through the north gate and across a gravel path by a capacious greenhouse, an immaculate formal garden to our right, we crunched towards the garden's midpoint. Extending east and west was a rather fabulous 90m crinkle-crankle.

"Last one," I said, placing a palm on the hot bricks. "Flippin' done it."

I imagined being reluctantly raised aloft, perhaps on Peter's shoulders, while the crowd roared, everyone flexing an arm to imitate a writhing snake. Instead, my wife flip-flopped off to examine the abundant choisya, my mum vanished through an opening to take commemorative photos destined for *Let's Talk* magazine, and Eldest & Peter were busy borrowing sunscreen from a nearby twosome: she had a yellow fleece around her waist, he wore a baseball cap. Realisation dawned when a gangly pre-teen loped into view. My nephew (crew member 6) had been dragged along by his mom & pop. About to join them, I heard somebody call my name and spun around to face an older couple.

"You're here too!" I blurted out to my in-laws. The day was turning into a US TV end of season finale in which all cast members, some of which you struggle to place, return to make a brief contractual appearance.

"Nice wall, that," observed my father-in-law in his Kookaburra cricket hat.

"You said it," I confirmed. "Years ago when West Brom were on a pre-season tour, they had an excursion to the Great Wall of China. Reporters asked the players what they thought, and one said, 'You've seen one wall, you've seen 'em all.'"

"They're a funny lot in the Midlands," he replied.

From beds of bear's breeches, assorted greenery had been trained like Sherpas to climb selected stretches of the red brickwork. Here and there clung an espaliered pear tree, clearly making the most of those warmer inner curves. Attempts to capture my own prizewinning images were thwarted by Middler's prolonged photobombing – she'd done the same back at Carlton Colville (#46) – preening by the pink peonies in her Aviators and cut-off dungarees. Lovely archways too, the weathered white keystones working well against some bloomin' red roses. Not to be outdone for colour contrast, the far side of the wall ran parallel to an entire runway of shoulder-high purple verbena. For something constructed in 1796, when Jane Austen was drafting Pride and Prejudice, this wall's in remarkable shape; mind you, I believe that all serpentines are a remarkable shape. Its condition is undoubtedly due to the close attentions and deep pockets of present-day landlord Jon Hunt who, together with designer Kim Wilkie, has been implementing Capability Brown's forgotten 1782 plans for the grounds. Like a Patek Philippe watch, you never actually own an original crinkle-crankle wall but merely look after it for the next generation.

Over the course of the day random familial permutations watched powerboats whizz around the lake, craned necks at the supercars (the so-called Concours d'Elegance) arranged on the curvaceous terraces behind the house, and appreciated the ladies and gentlemen ballrooming on the lawn by James Wyatt's 1789 orangery. Yes, they were dancing cheek-to-cheek. Around 4pm, still within sight of that wonderwall, a group of us (excluding the in-laws and Middler who were patronising the gin stand) retreated to the cool oasis of the tea tent. As we held our cups & saucers, a brass band tackled The Floral Dance, jasmine hung in the air, and, from our deckchairs, we squinted up at the red, white, and blue smoke of the RAF Falcons parachute team. Quite the sensory overload.

"So that's it?" said my mum, clearing the last crumbs of her malt loaf.

"For now," I said. "Serpentine House at Blyford seems to have gone and there's possibly one near Sibton that I can't pin down, but yep."

"Shame we didn't reach 100 walls."

"That Wikipedia page only ever claimed 50 or so. There's bound to be others. You never know what'll pop up on Rightmove, plus I still get the odd email. I'd say we've done alright, all in all."

"All in all, a lot of walls." She drained her cup. "How's your Sally Lunn?"

~~~ THE END ~~~

Acknowledgements

Thanks to Edward Martin from the Suffolk Institute of Archaeology & History for swapping crinkle-crankle lists, and to Dr James Bettley for sending me a customized extract from his comprehensively updated Suffolk books.

Lesley Dolphin generously invited me to broadcast my appeal on Radio Suffolk. I'm much obliged to her and the many listeners who responded.

Emails still arrive to suggest potential unvisited walls, which is great. I've tried to name all spotters within the text.

Owners of houses large and small invited me into their gardens, for which I'm grateful. Special thanks to those understandably bewildered folk where yours truly (and his mother) turned up uninvited on their doorstep.

I'm indebted to Paul Sutton-Reeves and his writing group – Adrian, Carol, Georgia, Jess, Kate, Louise, and Paul – for their plentiful feedback. As one of them inadvertently said, this story "is a kind of Suffolk Travelodge".

Love to all members of the Crinkle-Crankle Crew, badge or no badge.

Bibliography

Bettley, James & Pevsner, Nikolaus, *The Buildings of England – Suffolk: East*, Yale University Press, 2015

Bettley, James & Pevsner, Nikolaus, *The Buildings of England – Suffolk: West*, Yale University Press, 2015

Burns, Polly & Ranft, Tina & Surry, Nigel, *Walled Gardens of Suffolk*, Suffolk Gardens Trust, 2014

Florio, John, *An Encyclopaedia of Gardening*, 1822

Loudon, John Claudius, *A Worlde of Wordes*, 1598

Pevsner, Nikolaus & Radcliffe, Enid, *The Buildings of England – Suffolk*, Yale University Press, 1974

Scarfe, Norman, *Suffolk – A Shell Guide*, Faber & Faber, 1960

Sebald, W.G., *The Rings of Saturn*, The Harvill Press, 1999

Symes, Michael, *A Glossary of Garden History*, Shire Publications, 2006

Selected Articles

Burns, Polly, *'Crinkle-Crankle Walls'*, Suffolk Gardens Trust newsletter, 2005

O'Neill, Jean, *'Walls in Half-Circles and Serpentine Walls'*, Garden History, 1980

James, Trevor, *'Out and About Looking at Crinkle-Crankle Walls'*, The Historian, issue 101, 2009

Index of Crinkle-Crankle Wall Locations

www.ingramcontent.com/pod-product-compliance
Lightning Source LLC
Chambersburg PA
CBHW010856090426
42737CB00020B/3394